A Peach Tree
in the Projects

A Peach Tree in the Projects

*A Work in Poetry, a Work in Pictures,
a Work in Life, My Work, My Signature*

Geneva K. Olowoeshin

A PEACH TREE IN THE PROJECTS
A Work in Poetry, a Work in Pictures,
a Work in Life, My Work, My Signature

iUniverse books may be ordered through booksellers or by contacting:

iUniverse
1663 Liberty Drive
Bloomington, IN 47403
www.iuniverse.com
1-800-Authors (1-800-288-4677)

ISBN: 978-1-4917-9917-8 (sc)
ISBN: 978-1-4917-9918-5 (hc)
ISBN: 978-1-4917-9919-2 (e)

Library of Congress Control Number: 2016909242

Print information available on the last page.

iUniverse rev. date: 01/24/2017

Book Description

My book "A Peach tree in the Projects," is a book that has taken the very best I have of myself, and brought to life the poetry that exists in and all around me. Sometimes I've felt I've been writing it all my life.

My poetry reflects so much of what I grew up taking in. There were so many concerns during the post-civil rights era in the South. The Watergate situation bothered my sense nobility and, most of all, there was always the complicated emotions of not knowing who my natural parents were. I combined my complicated issues growing up with my present lifelong lessons and experiences.

I hope the reader can understand my rhythm.

When I began writing poetry, I had no intentions of one-day completing a book so the whole idea is a pleasant surprise to me. I found myself, while on this long journey, laughing, crying, praying, and many times, just feeling the relief wash through me with the healing power of words.

The more I grow toward the full circle of self-love and appreciation of life, I hope that this book will help others as we struggle with life, to just find your smile, and keep hoping for the best.

Geneva K. Olowoeshin

Author's Biography

Geneva Kate Boozer (Olowoeshin) was born, May 1964 in Atlanta GA. Although unsure of her original name at birth, she is confident that she was adopted from somewhere in Georgia at the age of 16 months. Her adopted Mom named her for her new Grandmothers, one who was very proud to be an integral sculpture to help mold in her the strength and love from her name (Kate). The other Grandmother for whom she would proudly carry her name was a complete opposite. She quickly changed her name to Genevieve.

She was raised in the heart of Atlanta with 3 other adopted siblings. She attended Collier Heights Elementary School and Frederick Douglass High School, and briefly attended The Atlanta Metropolitan Junior College in the late 1980s, only to be compelled to leave to explore new life experiences.

She began her writing career very early in life as required by true educators, and very demanding teachers and later, distinguished college professors.

The summer of 1988 proved to be a crucial time in Atlanta. As the city became scorched by the drug epidemic, Geneva and other city leaders worked together to create and organize the "Kids Against Drugs" parade and rally where city leaders could see the sad eyes of mostly young African American boys who just wanted to know how to shake their single Mothers out of the haze of 'crack-cocaine' addiction.

She soon moved with her family to Minnesota, Ohio, and now resides in Florida.

Geneva is the proud Mother of 4 young Men, and now 4 Grandchildren.

Geneva K. Olowoeshin

For my Family, everywhere

Contents

The Finale

Reflections of Today, Tomorrow, and Yesterday

POEMS;

Reflection
Mama Went to Sleep
This Friendship
Sunrise
Love and Life...Life and Love
Vision
This Morning
The Finalist

The Summation   Get?It

Me

I'm the one born, whom they chose to forget
I'm the one thrown away, or left on a doorstep
I'm the one to whom you said, "Hold your head high"
I'm the one waving to speak when going by
I'm the one someone gave up on, she didn't understand
I'm the one, the 'X' chromosome, from my daddy, a man
I'm the one, the baby, so alone and out of place
I'm the one, looking for kinship in every ones' face
I'm the one, the Southern Bell, the Georgia, the Peach
I'm the one, and this is my life sometimes bitter, sometimes
Sweet

G.O 1998

Me

(Analyzed)

I was inspired to write the poem "Me" after I had just walked around the artsy Santa Clara area in Dayton, OH which is about a block away from my residence.

It is an area that reminds me slightly of a place in Atlanta, a smaller mid-town perhaps Santa Clara, though, had something I found extraordinary. The art gallery.

This art gallery though, felt to have an exclusive air to it. It felt well respected with its pleasant scent of a type of canvas that was about to become a masterpiece. I liked this center piece in the art district in Dayton.

This art gallery also bears my grandmother's maiden name.

Of course when I first moved to this area, I went there, to the gallery, with lots of self- appointed privileged questions for the owner.

Although he was white and I'm only the adopted part of the name that ties me to the family, I searched his demeanor and mannerisms to find my father's and grandma's heritage within this meek and mild man.

I felt as though I had every right to announce to him and his burly son the fact that their name was a name that I had grown up with, and the stories I heard weren't always good. They both went out of their way to deny our possible kinship. They had no problems, however, when it came down to giving me a short history lesson about their heritage, proud, southern and as I listened I was so amazed at how so steeply intertwined our families were, right off the slave ship on the Carolina gateway. This only proved to me how much people wish to forget the atrocities of the ones who preceded them, as they didn't mention whether or not their family owned slaves.

Early one sunny afternoon, I went to the art gallery. I wanted to know if the picture that I had taken with my aunt's camera could be something that could be transformed into art. It was at an honors dinner for my son when I had taken the photo, and poetry explained it.

The owner came out to help me and for some reason, his gentle eyes were a comfort to me. I often get nervous when trying to explain my ideas. His eyes, though, seemed to say to me, "I understand you." I was able to explain my ideas with no problem. I know that he probably assists many people everyday, and I had only been there twice. But the way we talked to one another felt so familiar. I found myself thinking that he really might be a part of my family.

As I left, I thought to myself, "I'll probably never know."

On my way home, I reflected on the notion that even though we may or may not be related, we were resolved to the fact that there is always a possibility.

I know of no origin

From whence

I came

But still I

Love me just the same

I don't look back

Always ahead

And I thank my God

For my daily bread

'Cause if it

Wasn't for him,

Where would

I would be?

I wouldn't be no where

And not loving

Me

So when I look at my

Sons, each

One a prince

That's really something

Since

I

Don't know the origin

From whence I came

Still I know me just the same.

Still I know me just the same

G.K.B. 1993

Origin

My adopted parents never kept the fact that I was adopted from me. This fact created a huge problem for me, because not knowing one self's origin can sometimes make a person wonder about their true worth. I often found myself in the mirror for hours trying to see myself, or make myself look like some ones face. The outcome was always the same, nothing. Then the questions came. Why, why would she give away? Maybe it was my looks. Maybe I looked like someone she couldn't bare to see every day. Maybe there was something wrong with me. I began a thorough examination of myself. I was quite clumsy, and extremely hyperactive. But surely these were not reasons that I should be unwanted.

I became angry at my adopted Mother as she was definitely not a match. Being as how she was white, colored, Creole, and who knows what else about her own origin sense she too was adopted. She would get a laugh to herself when reminiscing how she marched right in with the white folks to the first showing of the movie, "Gone With the Wind' at the Grand Fox Theatre. All the while she would feel a sort of kindred to the coloreds who were forced to sit in the balcony. Being adopted herself; I would often stare at her, wondering if she had ever questioned her origin. It was a question I wanted to ask, but I never felt it was appropriate. My adopted Father did, however, have a rich and strong heritage. With a caramel hue, and naturally curly hair, I did all I could to look like him. I studied and imitated some of his mannerisms, even brushing my hair back. When people would say; "You look just like your Daddy". I could hardly contain myself with joy!

One year during my early teens, our family made one of our frequent weekend trips to Columbus, GA to visit our extended family. These little getaways were always a high light for me especially during the middle of my terrible teens. I felt close to my extended cousins, and always comfortable there. It wasn't unusual for the grownups to have an impromptu party with their friends, while on the stove cooked, a fresh

Members of Egleston's family
RECOVERY ROOM:
Mrs. BOOZER and her husband have adopted twins – a boy and girl, CEDRIC and CEDILIA. They are to be congratulated upon these new additions to their family. The Boozers now have four adopted children.

CEDRIC and CEDILIA, eight-year old twins who were adopted on August 6, 1969 by Charles and Dorothy Boozer.

10

Who Am I

I am black and white, and every color in between

I am rich and poor

I am, as I seem

To be right

To be wrong

To be weak, to be strong

Who am I?

I am young and old; I've done much to be praised

I've seen issues come and go

And many not raised

I've been the eye of the storm

I've been the one to reform

Who am I?

I am a parent giving birth; I am knowing my true worth

I've been bought; I've been sold

I am free, I am bold

Who am I

'1993'

11

Where Am I

Where am i

This is the question I ask

Finding myself

Is such a serious task

Loving myself, or who I thought I was

When the real of me emerges

I'll love me must

Because

Fight with myself, if that's what I must do

Don't give up,

Love will win, and that's

The truth

No matter how much I try

Still I wonder

Where am I

Geneva 1999'

Sometime After 1850

There was some folks, who looked at my Grandpa,
And this is what they said;
"Git to the backroom boy,
To eat yo' daily bread.
And hand me that silver spoon,
Here you take this wooden one...
And don't come out to
Show yo'self, 'til we desire to have some fun."

So Grandpa humbly went to the back,
Holding on to his
Wooden spoon...
And there he sat, deep in thought,
But nowhere near to gloom.

With his head bowed low,
He said a prayer, from a book of which he'd read.
As he asked God to help him hang on,
To hang on to that he thought was his last thread...

'Cause you see his dignity, and his life,
And his child, and, His wife...
This is what he asked God to protect.
So that bigotry and hate, they would learn to reject.
And one day soon, he too would sing a song,
About the free and the brave,
And the struggles that he must go through,
The struggles that would make him great.
But for now, he enjoyed his dish,
Hot and fresh from the kitchen.
They may have taken his silver spoon,
But they couldn't take his vision.

1998'

Brothers

LIFT ME UP BROTHER

AND I'LL LIFT YOU UP TOO

YOU WASH MY BACK

AND I'LL WEAR YOUR SHOES

A FRIEND I WILL BE

WHEN THERE ARE NO OTHERS

A FRIEND UNTO THEE

A FRIEND LIKE

A BROTHER

1997

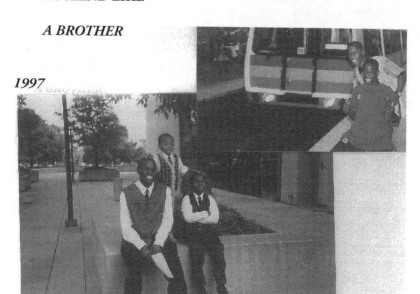

14

A Peace Tree in the Projects

My Grandmother lived in the projects in Atlanta, Ga. for fifty years. Beaver Slide projects were built in 1937. By the time my Grandma moved there in 1941, the projects were being re-built and re-named University Homes, as they were an added detail to the esteemed Atlanta University system. These projects were not a dead end ghetto, but a place where people could raise kids with an assured confidence in their surroundings. It was a place where a person's possibilities could seem endless, and their beginnings were as bright as the dazzling fireplaces left behind in the rural communities that encompassed the exciting city of Atlanta.

My Grandma was a strong sturdy woman. Her face was light and her hair was straight, and she never appeared to be the type of person who was ashamed of her African/Native American/Caucasian heritage. When I thought of her name being a part of my name, I believed I would be strong like her. Growing up, our family would spend our Sunday afternoons with Grandma. I remember seeing the neighbors on their porches preparing collard greens, or snapping pole beans as the summer's heat was the main topic of the day. We kids played outside while the adults talked and sipped a drink which we thought was water.

Grandma had been the caregiver for her deaf- mute sister and their aging Mother long before I was born. She had also lost a daughter when she was only sixteen. I often wondered as a child why Grandma didn't smile too much, but as I grew to understand the pains in life, I began to appreciate what my Grandma went through.

I could always identify with my Grandma. She was my pal. Before my parents adopted the twins, I can remember spending my days with her. I'd lie on the sofa at nap time while she would relax on her bed in the living room, which doubled as a bedroom. (The actual bedroom was filled with a lifetime of memories). We would talk about the family, (both living and not) and about the garden that she worked on almost every day, and which was very bountiful. I don't remember all that she told me, but I'm quite sure I've stored many of her stories to remember hopefully to tell my grandkids. I do remember walking to the church with her when she did volunteer work. She told me so many times to learn the books of the Bible and she even began to teach me. Whether watching her make lye soap, or helping her ramble through old clothes and pictures, we were like old friends. The toys she kept at her house were the greatest thing next to watching on her small black & TV "The Brady Bunch" while waiting for my parents to arrive from work. Then crawling to the back of the old station wagon to wave goodbye to Grandma. She would wave with both arms until we were out of sight. On a bright day, we could see her waving almost all the way to the end of Fair Street. That way it was fun leaving as well as arriving.

My Grandma and my Father got along pretty good, though I know it wasn't always like that. By the time I came along, I think they ere beginning a new chapter in their relationship. My Father had mellowed a great deal from his youth. Thanks to a thirty- year army commitment, which included two wars, and an even longer commitment to my Mom? (They were married 48 years at the time of my Fathers' death) My Father always had a relaxed and smooth demeanor. There were many things my parents could take or leave in this life, but what they had between themselves, many people want in their relationships today. Every family has problems that have hurt them, and ours is no different. My Mom tried to teach us that no matter what problems a person has to live with, whether in your family or in the world that you see, you must push on to find the right road.

Life to My Mom was a beautiful gift, something not to be taken for granted. While in Nagasaki, Japan after the first bomb strike ordered by Gen. Doolittle during World War Two, my Mother came to a deeper understanding of just how fragile life could be. Especially when life and the loss of life were decided on a man's decision to win or lose, to love or hate, to start or stop. In Korea, during that war, she waved to the prisoners of war as they left the infirmary on their way to whatever was next. Hopefully, she lamented later, to a place where they could learn to hate war and all its pain. The agonies of the wars they saw affected my parents in a most profound way. The direct contact with children

17

orphaned and parents left childless deeply touched my Mom especially. She told us that her heart broke when she was told that she couldn't adopt some of the children orphaned by World War Two. I think that's why she put so much hope into us. Even though all four of us were adopted, and many of Mom's friends criticized her for that decision, we still were raised to expect more from ourselves and all in our mist. We may not have been born with a silver spoon in our hands, but we were raised with the attitude that even the brightest star was within our reach. Our lives had been changed and molded by one single theory, love.

When someone planted a peach seed in my Grandmas' yard space in the projects, I know they hoped that it would grow and one day produce the fruit that Georgia is so well know for. By the time I was in my early teens, my parents, aunts, uncles, and cousins enjoyed the fruit born from this hope. As they all sat outside Grandma's door, maybe reflecting on the positive outcome from hard work and determination, I stood by. I didn't care what the old folks were saying, I was about to get a game of red light going. After all, playing in these projects was top fun at the time. A few years ago I went back to the place so familiar and dear to my heart. The tree has been cut down and the projects remodeled. The older ones are now gone. All that my Mother and Grandmother wanted for me became clear as the rain slowly blended with my tears of sweet memories that are priceless to me now.

Even though my Mom and Grandma came from different backgrounds and were related only through marriage, and they may not have been the ones who planted that peach seed, they both made sure that that peach seed had a chance to grow and succeed and see the beauty in it's worth...

A Peachtree in the Projects

Someone planted a Peach seed in the

Projects

With the hopes

That it would grow

Though small indeed

But nurtured well

It soon began to show

It laughed and played in summer breeze

Though warnings were

In place

That soon the ice and cold would freeze

The laughter on the face

But love of life was in the heart

Of the planter of that tree

And when rebellion

Swayed the branches

The planter set it free

Yes the planter was my mother

And she prayed

Since my birth

That someday soon this runt of a tree

Would find the beauty in her own worth

Learning 1

Hey old lady, tell me the truth

    I want to know all about the days

        Of your youth...

See I know yawl used to boogie down

    All that music, it's classic now...

Hush girl, let me study awhile

    And stop all them questions

You worrisome like a child.

I'm gon' teach you something all right

Young folks now days ain't too bright

The days of my youth wasn't that much fun

    I had babies to raise, and a house to run

Child, my man worked the field from sun up

    To sun down

We didn't go to the store for nothing, we could

    Grow from the ground...

You children, yawl got it easy today

Knowing we did a good job, that was most of our pay.

    And ya' lazy too...always want something for nothing.

Quit that shufflin' and jivin'...ain't you got something

    In the oven?

Poetic Pathways

Once, I flowed within a crowd

    As our paths parted

I was alone

    And wondering aloud.

                How I searched my true identity

                How I hoped someone would find me

                With my heart and head so strong

                I knew so much

Nothing could stop me...Nothing could go wrong

    Alas, troubles approached from

        All around

And finally I laid myself on the ground

    And I wept soft, yet independent tears...

How it rained, through my soul for so many years.

    When the sun came by to visit one day

I awoke, and the tears flew away...

Once, awhile back, I traveled alone

        As I thought I was lost,

    I reached out

        And poetic pathways led me home.

           G.O.1998

Sharing

There were   2   trains sitting all alone

    Looking so tired, but resting

      At home

No one asked them where they had been,

    They had seen a lifetime of

      Wear and wind...

So they sat there awhile, enjoying one

    Another, and when it was time to

      Leave

        They lingered...

      Because what they had shared was true.

G.O.1993

groWing

I looked into the eye of a richly lived

    But tired life

I saw hopes and dreams go sailing by

I looked into a love
Brand new

I saw sweetness like the morning dew

I walked on the road
Less taken

I understood why it had been forsaken

'G.O.1995'

GroWing

(Analyzed)

The poem, "Growing", depicts the inner most details of my life as I have watched and traveled along the road of being. In my life, I have enjoyed people (relatives) who are twice, and in some instances three times my age. When I write that I have looked into their lives, I am speaking of events that I have had the opportunity to share with these people that have shared themselves to mold and shape my life. I've seen hopes and dreams go sailing by, as some of these dreams have been fulfilled, while many have not. I find myself reflecting on the family joy I shared with my family shortly after arriving in Ohio, where I lived almost ten years. I was reunited with relatives that I have all my life. When one of my Baby Cousins' got married, I witnessed a love that was sweeter than any morning dew that I had ever known, or imagined. Their modest and fun reception made me reflect on the softness and endearing quality of what true love must be like.

On the other end of the spectrum, there is a road less taken. This road involves a path of depression. Writing about this road, helps me realize that although many of us have traveled this way, it still remains a road less taken. To me, it is a road that is to be avoided at all cost. However, if a person finds themselves' on this forsaken road, I suggest, from experience, smile, inside, and out...just smile, now, see what's next.

A Tree

IF I HAD THE OPPORTUNITY TO CONVERSE WITH A TREE
I'D SAY COME, UPROOT, TAKE A STROLL WITH ME

I'LL TAKE A NOTION TO UNDERSTAND YOUR POSITION
AND I HOPE YOU'LL RECOGNIZE

MY GROWING CONDITION

IF I TAKE A MOMENT, JUST ONE MOMENT SEE

I THINK I WOOD APPRECIATE YOUR NEED TO BE

THROUGH TIME AND SPACE, AND TRIALS
YOU FACE
YOU STAND AND WEATHER THE SEASONS
BUT WHEN I GO BY, I DON'T SEE WHY
YOU'VE LASTED SO LONG FOR SOME REASON

IN THE SUMMER, HOW THE CHILDREN
DO PLAY AROUND YOU!
AND NEVER WILL THEY QUESTION
YOUR PRESENCE...

AS CHILDREN LOVE TREES, I TOO CAN LEARN FROM BOTH,
MANY A VALUABLE LESSON

If Love is Wrong...
What's right?

Sometimes I wonder why my Parents wanted to adopt children. From examining their full lives, they had traveled extensively, and were close to age fifty when they got me. They had lived in Japan, and Korea, and many parts of the United States when it was my turn to know them. Just when their peers were ready to enjoy grandchildren, or the mid life freedom from raising kids, my parents were shopping for their children's first day of school.

My relationship with my Mom wasn't easy, to say the least. The enormous age difference always irritated me. I always felt sheltered and cut off from the fast pace that surrounded me. "Mama Boozer", for the kids who know and love her, didn't believe in keeping up with the "in crowd". While others may have found this to be an endearing trait, I despised it. I always thought I was missing something, so for many years, I rejected the protection that her shelter gave me. I thrust myself forward, only to recall these sheltering qualities in my later years that now make me thankful for her strong and unbending ways. No my Mom is no saint, and there are some things that I won't pass on to my kids, but when I realize the principles behind her methods, I am glad to have endured. In between all the struggles, we traveled, and became acquainted with the world around us. When I was age 9, my Father drove for a week to get the family to New Mexico to spend 2 weeks in a scouting camp. It was there that we experienced buffalo burgers, and climbed to the top of a mountain that seemed to touch the sky. These types of adventures made a lasting impression on my personal growth. Each summer, the family visited the South Carolina Island of Frogmore. With each visit, the ocean's view remains as vivid to me as the sounds of its harmonious waves in the many seashells my sister collected every summer. Every now and then, if I come across a fish market with the undeniable odor of the ocean, I truly find it difficult to leave. There were trips to apple orchards in the gay of fall. And escapades to the world of Disney during the winter school breaks. Our weekend visits with extended family always gave us a breather from the busy city life.

My life as a child was one of learning, and accepting that life is what a person makes of it. Most of all, I think I had a full understanding that life is full of options. Our parents may not have conceived us from the start, but they tried to teach us that love goes far beyond the conception. Although they weren't rich, they taught us that with each opportunity to love life, there comes a richness that is not to be forgotten.

When I composed the first poem to my Mother, I realized that all any of us really want is to be loved and appreciated. That's why I know, Love isn't wrong...It's all right.

My father in Japan during World War II

A photographer caught this picture of some of the now 26 abandoned children being cared for by the Elizabeth Sanders Home, Oiso, Kanagawa Prefecture, Japan.

Princess And Son

(Acme Photo)
Shown above is Princess Elizabeth holding her infant son, Prince Charles of Edinburgh, during christening ceremonies for the child. The picture is a radiophoto from London.

Shown above is Princess Elizabeth holding her infant son, Prince Charles of Edinburgh, during christening ceremonies for the child. The picture is a radiophoto from London.

IRONY 1948

RE THIS PAPER   THURSDAY, December 23, 1948   SHARE THIS PAPER

MY DAD IN JAPAN

A photographer caught this picture of some of the now 28 abandoned children being cared for by the Elizabeth Saunders Home, Oiso, Kanagawa Prefecture, Japan.

Princess And Son

Shown above is Princess Elizabeth holding her infant son, Prince Charles of Edinburgh, during christening ceremonies for the child. The picture is a radiophoto from London.

30

The First Poem I Wrote to My Mother

THERE ARE NO WORDS TO SAY
HOW I REALLY FEEL
NO HOLIDAY ON EARTH TO
CONVEY THAT MY LOVE IS
REAL

AS LIFE GOES ON DAY BY DAY
AND PRECIOUS MOMENTS GO
AWAY
MY LOVE FOR YOU MOTHER
IS FOREVER HERE TO STAY

GENEVA KATE

1978

Learning 2

G.O.1997

Mama, Mama, tell me what's real

Should I like a boy for his looks?

Or should I like him for the way he feel?

Girl...

You better go and set down somewhere

That's all them good looks, and that

skin so fair.

I'm gon' teach you something, and you

might not like what I say.

But if I do a good job, well, that'll be my pay.

My Grandpa worked from sun up to sun down.

Just so we wouldn't run his name in the

ground.

Leave them boys alone, while you still got a change.

Besides, what do you know about love?

And romance?

Don't you answer that, cause I don't want to hear it.

If you knew what I know, you wouldn't go near it.

Baby; take your time that's what my Mama always said.

Be sure you can feed yourself, before there's a baby to be fed.

And stop trying to be so fast; give yourself time to grow...

Loving yourself, now that's what will last.

And that's the you, you need to know.

Sheltered

SOMETIMES

    WHEN I SIT

       I CAN HEAR

          MY

             SOUL BREATHING...

SOMETIMES

    WHEN I'M STILL

       I CAN FEEL

          MY

             BODY SCREAMING

YEARNING...BURNING...TO BE TOUCHED...TO BE HELD

DESIRE

    TO

       BE...LOVED

          TO ESCAPE MY OWN SHELL

       FREE MY BODY...FREE MY SOUL

       THE BURNING HEAT...THE FREEZING COLD

       !JUST LET ME OUT!

             G.O.1997

A Friend

There was a woman

I used to know

She wasn't a friend

By choice

But every time she spoke to me

There was love in her voice
I don't know what

Life she led, in her younger

Day

All I know is the friendship

We shared

Will stay in my heart

For it can never be

Replaced

REMEMBERING DOROTHY JUNE
AND LUVENIA K. 1997

There's Something Different About Us
Class of 1982
Frederick Douglass High School

I had many hopes and dreams while growing up. As a matter of fact, I went to school with the sons and daughters of very important dreamers. The honorable King and Bond Families found my school to be one that the could instill hope and determination in every step that we made.

My teachers presented ideas that demanded leaders to step forward, no matter if afterwards they went home to the projects or the upper middle class neighborhood across the street from the projects. To the staff at FDH, I say THANKS.

The one thing I've always struggled with is leading me. I guess everyone has to learn to lead him or herself in a positive direction. Since we are so imperfect though, sometimes we find it hard to see ourselves as we really are.

I wrote the poem, "See Me", because I felt okay with inviting the reader to see me as I am or for whomever they perceive me to be. One day, I realized that we all have to view ourselves in a positive way; if that is the way we hope to be seen by others.

Of course our teachers and parents were consistent with discipline and stern about attention.

My pre-school through first grade were spent at a small private school named, "I Am Sanctuary" I really loved that school. The classes were made up of only 12-14 kids, and when the twins joined our family, their class was right next to mine. Sometimes I could see them in their 4th grade room from my 1st grade classroom. For some reason, even though I was still mad at them for becoming my brother and sister, I felt a bit more secure knowing where they were, and I had easy access to them. Our parents would drop us off at the front door, and when our parents got off work by 5pm, we were comfortable there in the after school care where we watched ULTRA MAN!!! Or played outside.

Our world was suddenly changed one morning while being the first to arrive usually, the head Mistress Mrs. Parker, was tragically in the throws of a massive heart attack. My sister calmly ushered her twin and myself away from that painful scene and we waited for other adults to arrive. Now our beloved Sanctuary had to merge with a more expensive school "Snow White" So the start of my second grade year, we began public school. I remember close to thirty kids giving me an unsettling look as intruder number 1. Later that year, we would be giving intruder numbers 2 and 3 the same look when they arrived. But right then I was terrified, and lonely. The twins, whom I was slowly warming up to, were in another section of this huge complex. I felt completely alone and abandoned. I stared through the windows trying to see the twins across the large courtyard with no success, and Mrs. Busby wouldn't allow me to keep going to the rest room as I would make a mad dash to the 5th grade hall to ask for my brother rather boldly. The last time I made it to him, we sat on the cool floor outside his class, and he tried to tell me not to be afraid, and try to be brave like him. I did not hear anything he was saying as I had already developed the idea to just walk out and go home. I pleaded with him to come with me, but he still had good sense then, and knew the out come would not be good. So, I made the decision without him. I took my lunch box, and left.

I was sure I remembered the way the bus went, and I was on my way. But the street looked different without the school buses. I went a little ways right, and a little ways left and finally ran to the woods where I could cry, and pee. After I gained my courage again, I began my trek out of there, but a man just appeared from nowhere. He looked dirty, but kindly asked if I was going to eat my lunch. I liked neither mustard nor bologna so I gave it to him. We sat there a while as I told him my plight. He guided me to the street where he flagged down a motorist, and told the woman where to take me. For some odd reason, I felt no fear or trouble as the kind lady dropped me at our next door neighbors' home. I ran straight to the swing set as Mrs. Wilson went in to call my Mother, who promptly drove at break neck speed to collect me while I remained clueless to what was about to occur. I got a rude awakening on the way back to school. When she asked why, I said I didn't know. I was soon introduced to the back of her hand across my nose. That's when I realized what the switches were for in the back seat. I knew why I left school I just could not verbalize it. When she held me by my dress and switched me for what seemed like hours in front of the class, it became a major event in the public school system in Atlanta which I don't think has been topped yet. She then proceeded to frighten the class with a threat that she would do the same to them, gave the teacher a scary glare, then marched to the office and threatened them with lawsuit for losing a child. My new school had to be my pride now.

By the third grade we were all comfortable with each other, but wasn't too sure about our white teacher who, for some of us was the 1st white woman to command our respect and attention. Ms. Robinson was tough and I must have mistaken her marshmallow looks for softness. I was bad. Everywhere she put me to stop me from talking; I still was able to start a group discussion or debate, depending on the group of course. Thus came up the question of color which seemed to get more passion from me than all else. While the lighter colored classmates made fun of the darker ones as our geographical textbook displayed uncivilized jungle pictorials, I was quick to ask why, if the jungle was so black, white or light Tarzan came on television every Saturday swinging and screaming with the whole jungle as his friend. One day Ms. Robinson got so tired that she sent me to the hall to wait for her discipline. Surprised as I am to have remembered this, that's how surprised I was when she came out and began to shake me. I guess she was trying to shake and knock some sense into my head because I tried to stop talking as much as I could, but it didn't work. I didn't settle down in this grade until the spring when she began reading, "Charlotte's Web" I loved that book so much until I checked it out from the library and never brought it back. Sorry.

By the fourth grade, I was playing violin in the orchestra, "What the World Needs Now, is Love Sweet Love" was my favorite line from a song, and Mrs. Cook was calling the whole class heathens, and whacking me and others across the back with three rulers taped together when needed. My classmates then, joined together with a few other local elementary schools to make up the class of 1982, and yes, there was definitely something different about us. In 1977 when about to graduate to the 8th grade to high school, integration was a hot issue. My Mother firmly opposed this along with other parents. Their logic went like this; Let those white kids integrate to our schools and soak up some of our culture. Why should our kids have to travel forty-five minutes there when we had perfectly good schools right here.

I think maybe 1 kid tried it, but it didn't last. We had white teachers, mulatto classmates, but for some reason, integration did not work for us. I didn't care; I had my own anger issues to deal with. Kids picked at us for everything from being adopted to having a Mother who would show up and embarrass us at any time. Plus, our school clothes were bought from the cheapest stores in town, and it seemed like everyone knew this. But we made it to graduation, which was the normal process of our educational careers. The armed forces and college were not for me as I had to go on a valuable search for something special and precious to only me. MYSELF.

And Now, Introducing...

THE BEATING

A 1971 Atlanta Public School

Event

The day my mama beat my ass
In front of the class
The sun was shining bright
I ran away from school
It just felt fight

To leave
To walk away
From what I did not like
Public school
Learn the rules
Stay in school!

                         Stay in school!!

                                    Stay in school?????

Why Geneva Kate why,
Why did you leave??
ANSWER ME!!!!!!
I miss the privacy of private school
I thought...

                         I spoke; "I don't know"

SLAP!!!!   Right across the bridge of my nose
Blood flowed like a red, red rose
I DON'T KNOW, I DON'T KNOW I DON'T KNOW

I cried, I lied, because public school should have been my pride

So I lied

The switches in the back seat laughed at me

I glared at them

Wanting to set them free

But now... we were back at school

And the creole was determined to show me the rules

In front of the class

On the carpet even

She held me by my checkered dress and

Switched me, confused me, and

Beat my ass in front of the class.

I screamed, kids laughed, teachers gasped

                              Too many moments passed

                                     The beating

                              And upon leaving

                    I lay there demolished and bleeding

                    I looked up to see the long silk platte

          Swing around...she glared at the snickering class

             And growled, "The same will happen to you"

One kid peed, one kid cried, teachers shook their heads

In disgust...   and finally ...   I felt pride...The Beating

Geneva K. Boozer

41

Dreaming

"I HAVE A DREAM"

That's what one man said
He believed in that dream
And was shot in the head
I was dreaming

When we cut down the trees
That we dearly loved
First we pushed

Then we shoved
In my dream

Ohio 1997, Veterans Hosp.
Expanding burial space

My Daddy is a veteran
Vietnam is the war
He gave his life
Just because we were poor
By the time he did see
The world

He couldn't approve
The things,
Terrible things

2 wars told him to do
By the time I was growing up
My Daddy could understand
Why my love

Stretch far across the oceans spans

G.O.1997

Before The Twins

After The Twins

Thanks

Thanks to the teacher, for banging
My head on the wall
Thanks to the yardstick that whipped
Me in the hall
Thanks to my Mom, for being so ruff
Thanks to that discipline, I keep on pushing
When life gets tuff
Thanks to my high school, for putting pride
In my hand
To all my teachers, thanks for making me stand
Thanks to my Father, who served his country well
If I ever need welfare, I won't feel like I've failed
Thanks to my birth mother, who gave me up
For adoption, Thanks to the mom who raised me
And showed me my options.
Thanks to true friends, even those who were fake
Thanks for teaching me to give, more than I take
Thanks to my husbands and lovers in life
Thanks for believing I could be a
Good wife

Commencement Exercises

Of the

FREDERICK DOUGLASS

HIGH SCHOOL

Atlanta, Georgia

Commencement Exercises
of the
FREDERICK DOUGLASS
HIGH SCHOOL
Atlanta, Georgia

FREDERICK DOUGLASS
HIGH SCHOOL

Suffer No More

SUFFER NO MORE
RICH AFRICAN AMERICAN
THE WHIP DON'T WHISTLE
AT YOUR BACK NO MORE
DON'T BE AFRAID, AS YOU
LET YOUR WINGS SOAR

SUFFER NO MORE
RICH AFRICAN AMERICAN
THE WHITE IVORY NO LONGER
RULES YOUR LIFE
THE DAY IS SHORTER NOW
HURRY HOME TO YOUR WIFE

SUFFER NO MORE
RICH AFRICAN AMERICAN
AS BEAUTY ENTRANCES YOUR NAME
A LONG WAY YOU'VE COME BABY
YOU'VE SURELY EARNED YOUR FAME
AND THOUGH THERE ARE CHILDREN
HUNGRY SOMEWHERE
IT'S YOU THAT'S BEGUN TO GROW
SUFFER NO MORE RICH AFRICAN AMERICAN
AS YOUR LOVE BEGINS TO FLOW

G.O.'99'

Suffer No More

I wrote this poem, not only to answer and respond to Mr. Hughes' poem, "Suffer Poor Negro", but to think of and reflect on how far people had come. People from all races have grown and advanced in humanity just from the courageous acts of those who lived before. Understanding this concept means that I must do all that I can to promote what is true and beautiful, and kind, and loved. The poem, 'Suffer No more', not only identifies me as a part of a generation who grew up watching adults deal with freedom, and how to treat and be treated by their fellowman. I was also a child still seeking answers as to the way people chose to appreciate life, or not. I finally felt ready to say, "Suffer No More" rich, rich, African American. You've combined your resources. You have taken the best of the best, and reached for more. You've made mistakes, and many have given up. But when I go out and see a well fed man. His beauty makes me smile. Men with mustaches, some need to shave. Men with thick hair, braided hair, some need to be cut. A man prone to smile or a man whose brow makes him distinct. Light skinned, or as dark as the sweetest night sky, with stars for teeth. Plain or extremely laid back, with a style that makes you want to recite poetry on the spot. A man in all his annoying, and mind boggling, boasting and endearing sass that make you want to kiss all night. (And some daydreams that make the soap opera goop look like a fading stench).

Yes, men of many races have spoken to me, and given me directions, changed my car starter, sold, and bagged my groceries, shook my hand, told me a joke, sold me a vehicle, watched me as I drove in traffic, married me, and tickled me, and just been my friend. From my Father on, I can say, that even though man is not perfect, there have been some who had tried. And I have met a few in my life that left me terribly disappointed at times. But when I consider the struggles between mankind only a few generations before my birth in the 1960's, the struggles in that generation alone should have me want to curl up in my mother's womb and stay put. At least until the calm had rested. I guess love just couldn't wait. As I emerged into a world of Negroes and coloreds, my bald head, like newborn white baby must have startled my mother, and she took this little mixed, candy apple dipped in caramel baby to her rightful owners. They turned out to be the creole, and half and half Georgia folk, who knew what to do, and with the grace of God, they raised me, and set me free.

Though battered and torn, I have always known that I have a man to lean on. Whether brother, husband, friend, son, or Father, there is always a man to hold my hand when I'm not quite so sure of my own beauty. To you Men...and boys to Men...You have my Love.

Suffer No More...Rich African and American

As your love continues

To flow.

'1999'

My Buddy

MY BUDDY DIED OF AIDS

OH YES HE DID

SOMEONE STOLE HIS MANHOOD WHEN

HE WAS JUST A KID

IT WANNT MY PAW

OH NO IT WAS NOT

IT WAS SOMEONE ELSE

WHO SOMEHOW FORGOT

LIFE

IS WAS WE MAKE OF IT

AND NONE OF US HAS THE RIGHT

TO STEAL FROM ONE

ANOTHER OUR PRECIOUS

GIFT OF

LIFE

My Buddy

(Analyzed)

This poem is about my adopted brother, Cedric. He was my best friend, and came with a twin sister. I don't remember when he became my best friend. One day I was brooding over the fact that my parents had gone and adopted 2 more kids, (who had the nerve to be older than me) to what I would wear on the day of my first day in 6th grade. Cedric let me wear his bell bottomed, plaid, cuffed slacks. It was the current fad for boys or girls back then.

Well, needless to say, I was a hit. The "in crowd" marveled at my fashion sense so much so that I didn't care that my butt was whipped when Mama found out that I was wearing boys' clothes to school.

I don't know when me and Cedric were classified as the rebels in the family, but as soon as we had a sense of the thought, we did all we could uphold that reputation.

One year Mama decided to ban everyone from drinking anything except water. I was okay until me and Ced. Saw her stocking piling 2 liter containers of 7-up for her guest and company. Once we realized that 7-up looked just like water, we both figured that if we drank only a little, and replaced it with water, no harm would be done. We didn't count on was the monumental fact that when kids get home from school, they are extremely thirsty. By then, water was so far beneath us, and we were "the water replacement agents" (WPA) until Mama's company eventually stopped by. We saw the always simmering volcano that we called 'Mama' about to erupt. Her company shamelessly evaporated, as Mama called us each by name, we wanted to evaporate. Oh, how I remember the fear of being exposed. I denied it all, and Cedric did the same, because we had a secret code of silence to protect us. We forgot one more thing though. His twin sister. She knew of our thievery, even warned us more than once. She hesitated not to reveal our secret although she only did so when mama threatened to punish all for the crime that one or two had committed. Out of the corner of my eye, I saw Cedric fold with his tell, the twice rub from his forehead down his nose. I never could get angry when he folded because we always shared the blame.

Its memories like these that make me laugh when I'm thinking of my 'buddy', Cedric. His life had been so hard from the beginning. Someone had tampered with his manhood before he could understand that far in life. I cried and cried when he died of aids. The pain stretched out in my heart, as I wept deep tears of my grief. I grew angry at anyone who didn't understand what it must be like to be homosexual. It was a life of confused affliction for my 'buddy'. I begged of myself to interpret the life, the language with empathy. It was not easy. My anger turned on me, and I found myself in a dark place with only sparkles and loud music, party music. Life was a constant party even when there was no party. Some drugs were there to help me find the easiest way to hate the beauty of who I was. How I wanted all who hated what they were born to be to awaken from that path of this type of depression. To have a new reality. But my hopes are dashed, for since 1988, I have cried. As that path has become the norm, the fad, the way to be. Many embrace this life as they murder what was created, not by them, but for them.

So as more than 20 years have come and gone, my eyes are still filled with tears for my Brother-Cedric Fern Boozer, April 3, 1961-May 22, 1988.

North and South...And Now the Two Shall Love

I've lived 4 major cities in my life. I've learned to appreciate and enjoy each one for its' own unique flavor and special beauty.

As a child, in the seventies, I remember my parents taking us to the visit the Fabulous World of Sid and Marty Croft in the newly built Omni complex close to downtown Atlanta. During the winter holiday season, the Omni ice skating rink would host our elementary school orchestra. (I've play the violin since I was eight) We would play along with recorded music as enthused nearby skaters seemed to glide on the ice. They looked to me to be dreaming of accolades and applauses as their elegant dancing lit up the ice. I remember going to Hawks basketball, and Braves baseball. Memories of being in the crowd as Hank Aaron reached goals that seemed impossible, and how the fireworks that followed amazed the child in everyone there. Then there was the freedom of relaxing on top of the old station wagon as airplanes soared right above us. We would imagine all sorts of places the passengers were coming from or going to. Many times I was frightened because my Father always drove us to a spot where the planes seemed to be about to land right on top of us. We had plenty of church going and camping trips while growing up. Both of which instilled a wonderment and realization of the one who entrusted us humans with so much. We visited Buck head, and Stone Mountain, GA, places that seemed too small to me, but full of that old southern scenery that makes the south so special.

Then, there was Minnesota, where the snow became my friend. In the winter of 1992, me and my three year old played and munched on the fresh fallen and knee deep snow like it was the best season of our lives. It was in MN that I began a deep search of myself. I started on my quest to learn to really love myself. I realized that I would have to push myself beyond what was expected of me. Sometimes my life felt like a trap, making me see myself through one angle. I had to push myself beyond what I expected of me. This included letting go of all my preconceived notions that left me empty and in want of heart. Always looking, yet never satisfied with my inability to grow.

By the time I arrived in Ohio, I had a clearer understanding that I must find my best angle, and bring it into full focus. Learning to appreciate and not condemn what had to be improved to find success in my personal growth process. It was in Dayton where I was forced to slow down, and pay more attention to my own self worth.

Now here in Florida, I think that in each place I've lived, and grown, I've taken a little something and made it a part of my own special personality. In my hometown, Atlanta, I've watched how small surrounding towns added flavor to that main city's success. In St. Paul, I met people who loved me for what I carried inside, and only saw brightness in my spirit. In Ohio, I miss my many cousins and aunts who always made me feel needed, loved, and welcomed.

Yes, there were times when we'd laugh at each other's accents. But as we looked deeply into our similarities as people, and found a common threat and hard and fast tests bond keeps us growing. This belongs to all people.

I haven't been far north for any length of time, but the mid west and the south, and all the places in between have taught me one valuable point. We all have something to offer each other...The Best of Ourselves, in the North or South.

Where

By

Geneva Olowoeshin

I have been to
Africa
Can't you see?
I went to Africa
When I looked at
At me

I really have
Ben to
Africa
Don't you know?
I belong to Africa,
Me and my beau

I've been to Africa
Well,
Not literally
I
Am Africa
For Africa is a part of
Me

G.O. '96

I'm Not Mad

I'm not angry

        Let me tell you why

If anger had a name

            It would drift away

           The sky

I'm not mad

     What I see is good

All colors share the

        World

Do we share what?

          We should????

I'm not angry   Judge me not

      And don't forget

        We have all been

Wrong

    We all have regrets.......

                    I'm Not Mad

For history has

    Already been foretold

The good   the bad

    The young

    And

    The old

                        '1997

Georgia in Saint Paul

I remember living in a place like this

Where you look

Out

And see the skyline

And fish frying

A beautiful rainbow

The baby cries

'1997

Years Later in Florida

Living with an older Son of mine

    Staring at a rainbow feels just fine

Something so familiar about this scene

    Let's me know it's not from a dream

The only thing missing

    The smell of catfish

        Frying on the stove

    And just when I settle in the moment

        The baby cries

    Again

    Only this time he's on

The phone, tells me what

    A bad day he's had

Figures like I pat him on the back

    I tell him

I'm sorry that he's sad.

    Then we go to eat,

    Tacos.

2011

Sometime After 1915

There were some folks, who looked at my Father,
And this is what they said;
Let's take him out of the cotton fields,
Put some book sense in his head.
We'll send him to private schools in places like Boston and New York,
And give him the same chances we have, and let him play in our sports.

And though there are some who won't like this at all,
We'll stand by our decision; we'll help that boy stand TALL

'Cause you see, one day we looked at ourselves
And we didn't like what we saw...
To deny someone the basic needs in life
Is such a serious flaw.
So we'll set ourselves on this quest to do the right thing
And no matter what becomes of this
Our praises we will sing

And our fore parents, no we won't be like their kind
We'll abandon the slave mentality,
A new day we will find
So that hopefully one day, we ALL can learn to forgive...
ALL of the pain that we have caused
Throughout ALL the generations we
Have lived

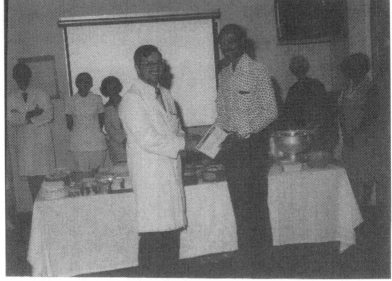

63

Conversation

Some of the things I've wanted to do

I've done

Some of the races I've wanted to win

I've run...

>>> And some chicken, Girl I don fried!
>>> And chitlins too, mmmm, you ain't never lied

>> Oh, how we could see as far

> As the eye could see

And the fields we worked

> Now that wasn't no small feat!!

And the man I loved; now that was pure beauty

I must say that...Ya'll didn't hear me,

> Let me reiterate that fact...

This was a MAN!!! And we grew together, you see.

I believed I loved that Man the first time he saw me.

>>> And could sing!! Oh, we made it beautiful

>>> Together

>> You know he stood by me in the most tumultuous

Weather

But love wasn't much to brag on then, you know

'Course we understood the truth in

You reap just what you sow

Yes sir, we stayed together through

Thick and thin

There, that's his picture, look at that

Fat little chin

Wait a minute...That's me

Well, like I said

There are many days I won't soon forget

And many things I won't regret...

Whether running through the fields,

Or being content with life's choices

No I never had caviar, and I cringe at

The idea of oysters

Some of the things I've wanted to do, I've done

And some of the races I've wanted to win, I've run

1997

It was I, yes I, who looked to yonder

And Wept
Your beauty to refine
So well kept

How my heart does leap
When thy beauty does greet thee

And words are here
Yet calmly elude me

Often and much do I sit in despair
Hoping that with each turn
I will not despise thee

For that will be the day when my heart
Will remember not the song
That
Teaches thee to love

Untitled

(Analyzed)

The day I wrote this poem, (for which I have not been able to title) the air was warm and a bit muggy for an October day. As I usually enjoy the effects of the seasonal changes on the entire atmosphere, my attention was suddenly drawn to notice one particular tree that stands in the schoolyard near my home. I gazed at the tree as though it was my first time seeing it. The truth is, ever since I moved to this area in the winter of '96, I made a special effort to take notice of this splendid display of fall's natural course.

While gazing at this wondrous view of loveliness, its beauty, much too exquisite for words, I found myself close to tears. In my heart, I wept for something so beautiful, and so free. In all my travels and adventures, had I ever been so stunned by something so simple, yet so breathtaking? I pondered and searched my vocabulary for an explanation. At the time of my rediscovery of this natural phenomenon, I scolded myself for not having my camera with me. By the time I did return with my camera, the leaves had already begun to fall, thus the moment had past. Though disappointed, I searched for something that would bring about the visual emotions and heartfelt appreciation I had experienced before.

Fortunately, I soon made a trip to my Parent's home in Florida. On the border of Florida and Georgia, there is a lake that I always see at sunset when traveling through. This time, I did have my camera and I was pleasantly surprised when the pictures came out and to me, conveyed the same wondrous view of beauty I experienced while gazing at the breathtaking sight near my home.

So now, anyone who reads this poem can see why I looked to yonder and wept...

G.O.'99

The Importance of Color

What color are you? More importantly, don't you think it to be exceptional that we don't have a choice? No matter what color we are wrapped in, we have a fascination with any color that isn't ours. My friends told me once that they had worked with, or around people who had never had the opportunity to meet and befriend anyone outside their skin wrapping. These people, in turn were raising their children in the same type of insolated environment. This notion tickled me inside as my family was so mixed until I considered people in different wrappings as the happiest and needed condition to make this an interesting and, beautiful world. My first cousin, who was also named after our Grandmother, was as white to me as my Mother, and Grandmother was. The woman who raised my Mother, and to whom I owe part of my name, was as white as the whitest sheet I've ever seen. That was before she would hit her face with this enormous powder puff that made her look like a shriveled up white raisin, I think, or imagined.

In the third grade the darkest wrapped kids were being harassed by the lighter colored wrapped kids in class. All the while, I remember that our social studies book had displays of half naked dark wrapped natives in Africa swinging from trees. Uncivilized. That was alright with me until we got to the display of lighter wrapped people in Australia with clothes on. Civilized. The contrast disturbed me. My classmates couldn't help but began their own civil war. I was right in the middle, being a bit of both, and loving the beauty in all of our wrappings. Naturally I sided with my darker wrapped friends. I don't know why, but it seemed like the darker wrapped ones needed my support the most. They looked ragged and torn to me, like they had a heavier load in life than the lighter ones. The lighter wrapped ones were elegant, beautiful, and stronger somehow. That was in 1972, in the south, and I'll never forget the ragged, tagged group I sided with.

We all managed to go on through our first and secondary school career together, forgetting those silly, yet strange days. I remember looking from one group to the other and wondering," How do people dislike the color of each one's individual wrappings" I imagine that the oceans floors look like us, without a choice.

Black and White

Black is beautiful

White is too

I saw your beauty when

I looked at you

Why is it you can't see?

You're beautiful

In whatever color

You came to be

Why is it you deny?

We're all beautiful

In Gods' eye

Why is it you ignore?

Our colors lace

The ocean floor

White is beautiful

Black is too

Look at yourself

And see that its' true

Sept.'97

Superstitions

Why do people knock on wood?
Does it keep them from doing
The things they should?
Some folks are scared of
The black on a cat
But all cats act the same
When the hear the word, "scat"
Superstition, that's all it is
Sounds like a jingle
Plop, plop fizz
A broom, a ladder
Salt a shoulder to scatter
Somebody tell me
What the hell does it matter!
Seems to be a silly game
For we are just people
With a life to frame
I think it began with a legend
And a myth
No doubt about it,
Superstitions make us drift

G.O.'97

73

How Do We Forgive

How do we forgive...?

When we do not understand

What it is we forgive for

Do we forgive for hatred?

Or death, or life?

Do we forgive by living

In constant strife.

How do we forgive...?

When we do not even care

For what we have been given

Do we forgive for love,

Or joy, or peace?

Do we forgive by rushing

Our lives to cease

How do we forgive...?

When it seems to be

No good

Why do we relax when

We don't see a "hood"

A "hood"? One might ask

Yes, to hide the anger,

The pain, the fear

And all the evil thoughts

We carry all year

Now the "hoods" removed,

Evil exposed all the time

No one has a need to be

Loving and kind...

Desperation and despair

Lurk in every place

Misguided children show

The pain on their face

If ever a time for

Forgiveness, it's now

For now is the time for

Us to learn how...

Now is the time,

Before it's too late

Before we are totally

Consumed by our own

Self-hate

1989

My Neighborhood Nightmare

I almost stepped on a

Crack pipe today

But a kid got in the way

I grabbed him back

His eyes were black

There wasn't nothing I could say
I called to his Mama

Down the street

My voice was mute
She couldn't speak
This drug!!! The drugs!!!

This drug...

This drug is the villain

Could someone spare
A million x's a million
So to can get this stuff out off reach!!!
1987-1988; A very bad year at the A.T.L.

KGB1988

Sometime after Yesterday

There was some folks who looked at me,
And this is what they said...
We're so glad we did right by her Father,

And stopped sleeping in her bed.
We're so happy that her Grandpa prayed

That we would see the error in our ways.
And her Father helped open doors,

Changed attitudes that clouded his days.
And though we don't always understand,

Just what it is she wants.
We're thankful that we eased our conscience,

And ignored ignorant taunts.
'cause you see when everything is all said and done

We too have records to set and so many
Races to run.
Because one day we did recognize our main problem

The need to control with hate just made us
Feel rotten. And though there are many in the world,
Who never did change their hearts,

Their Children and grandchildren did not neglect their part...
As now as we sit back and watch this African/American grow and live,
We do appreciate her strong capacity to love and forgive.

1988

Ode to Africa

Ode to you, Dark Continent
Your beauty lies within

Don't ever stop to wonder
If your beauty is a sin

Ode to you, sweet continent
Your place is near the sun

Your texture like a rainbow
Through earth your heritage runs

Ode to you, Plaines of Serengeti
Your freedom alive relates

Man can never cease you
Man can never berate
Ode to you, sweet land of Africa
Greed has come and hurt is true
Still your love continues on
And your skies stay over blue

Ode to you, my home, my heart
To your rivers flow waterfalls
And desert storms stir heavy winds
As I hear my homeland call

Olowoeshin'98

Writing is Easy,
Everything Else is Hard

I've been writing and doing public speaking since I learned to speak. I've also been biting my nails that long too. I am basically a very nervous person. But something happens when I am speaking publicly. I can lose myself as my audience cheers me on. I approach every opportunity to speak like I owe the listeners the best of myself. The same can be said of my writing. I never grow tired of editing and re-editing. These gifts make me want my audience to have something to not only enjoy, but to grow from, as we travel through our poetic road together. I am confident that people will enjoy my performance as I was trained to speak correctly at all times. Whether reminding us to speak up when addressing someone, or just to stand properly, we were taught that there must be a standard of self-respect that we had to adhere to, always.

When I faced tough challenges while growing up and my parent's rules seemed unduly strict and definitely old fashioned. Reading was my escape. And since I wrote everything in my journal or to other relatives, which somehow got back to Mom anyway, life was an interesting and constant struggle.

Through it all though, I'm able to learn to live by many valuable lessons. One such lesson involves choices. These choices make us stronger, or they can sear our lives and conscience with regrets no matter what our station in life may be. And no matter where we are from, we look for that special someone to build us up and help to keep us smiling. As I keep graduating from one hurdle to face another, I do appreciate a pat on the back, and at times a voice to say "well done". I have to admit that I have to be the one offering this encouragement to myself sometimes.

My Grandmother taught me to enjoy the company of my elders, and these are ones that, in most cases haven't esteemed to the high society that beacons to so many to most often disappointment. The people I've grown and learned from have told me how to be content with choices that teach us how to live properly.

It is to these beautiful lighthouses that I give, "My Tribute."

Locked Down

THERE ARE GUARDS TO WATCH OVER ME

ALTHOUGH I DO NOT NEED THEM

THERE ARE BARS TO KEEP ME INSIDE

ALTHOUGH I DO NOT SEE THEM

WHEN I WAS

OUTSIDE

AND LOOKING IN

MY HOPES WERE FOR A DAY

WHEN THERE

IS NO SIN

NOW I AM LOCKED DOWN

WHERE IS MY HOPE?

IT IS IN THE UNNOTICED FLAG

WHEN THE WIND PUSHES IT

TO AND FRO

OR WHEN THE WIND REFUSES TO MOVE IT AT ALL

YET I KNOW THE WIND SURROUNDS IT

THIS FLAG

IT IS IN MY SON'S VOICE WHO KNOWS OF MY

STORY

AND THINKS OF MY BRAVERY

IN THE WEE HOURS OF THE NIGHT

IT IS IN THE TEARS THAT FLOW FROM MY

BOSOM

LIKE THE RAIN

ON AN APRIL MORNING

IN MY MEMORIES

MY HOPE SINGS OF MY STAND

FOR WHAT IS RIGHT

AND TRUE

AND NATURAL

MY HOPE IS ALL THAT I HAVE

LOCKED DOWN
01-17-99
G.O.
DAYTON, OH

Locked Down
(Supplemental Journal)

When I was locked up on the 11th of January, and shortly thereafter realized the seriousness of the charges, I began to keep a journal. The only papers at my disposal were the jail request forms. I decided that since I was keeping a journal, I might as well write the whole story. This, along with writing out emergency power of attorney forms for my cousin and friend to have access to my bank accounts, is how I spent the first few days behind bars. In order to keep from separating my boys, my friend moved herself and her 2 daughters to my house. All I could think about was the fact that there was now a house full of teenagers, (hers and mine) and my baby (age 5) pulling at her at once. I knew that she was not at all ready for such a situation to be thrown in her lap. I worried about this, as well as what would happen to me in this place where I was forced to wait to be extradited to Florida to stand trial. I prayed always for my friend to be strong enough to handle the burden of all these kids who were probably just as uptight as we were during this ordeal.

Whenever I feel consumed with life's problems, I look back at the jail paper that I spent so many hours with. And I smile, because I can be worried about things I can do something about. Now as I do mundane things, opening and closing the refrigerator. Forgot something again, open and close. Take a break, go relax on my waterbed.

Locked Down
(Journal Entry)

January 11;
Tricked by the job, and the bull in me is raging!!!!!!!! But my rage is trapped in a small cell in a small town in Ohio. Only my oldest child was awake when I left this morning-who knows when I will return. Some trumped up charges from 1996 in Florida between my Mom and me. Now settled, but not really says the charges-God help me... God help me........

(The Story)

In May of 1996, I decided to make the boldest move of my life. The decision I made involved my two oldest sons who had been adopted by my parents, and had lived most of their lives with them in Florida.

In 1984, my parents sold our family home in Georgia and purchased a smaller home in Florida for health reasons concerning my Father. My Father enjoyed twelve years with the Boys. He passed away in his sleep in winter of 1992. This left my Mother alone to care for the Boys, who in 1996 were 14 and 12 years old.

Previously, my Mother and I had a pleasant relationship, as our main concerns were the children. However, after my Father's death, she began to dislike my wanting to visit her and the kids. It got so bad until one year she called the police to have me removed from her property. I was in the middle of telling her of my plans to move closer to them and help her with the Boys. I was crushed by the experience, and I went back to Minnesota (where I was living during that time) sad and humiliated. I decided to give up on seeing my kids again. I got so depressed that I ended all communication between us, but they were always in my heart and thoughts.

Locked Down
(Journal Entry)

January 12;
I've cried all day. I blame myself. I gave up on myself once, now I feel like doing it again. But my baby keeps calling for me. My dreams are horrible and I fear for my boy's safety. I fear for my own safety. I will keep trying to serve God. I sing to Jah, my God.

(The Story, 2)

In November of 1995, my oldest brother visited my Mother with his family from their home in Texas. When he called me and told me of the situation there in Florida, I was forced to make life altering choices right then. He informed me of the terrible condition he had witnessed, and the horror stories he was told and made to swear not to reveal the source.

Both of my sons were on medication for behavioral problems. My oldest hit and threw things at my Mother, and sadly spent time in a mental hospital to calm his angry disposition. At the end of our conversation, my brother warned me that if I did not act, soon, I would have to bury my son for hurting our Mother. I was upset, but understanding of the situation that was escalating to an environment out of control. At the time of this conversation, I was just moving into my new apartment in Dayton, Ohio. My two baby boys and I had just moved away from Michigan where my 2nd husband, (baby boys Father) had once again abused us and left me no other alternative but to leave. Not wanting to go back to Minnesota or Georgia, We set out for the place where I felt I would have the support of family. Our only possessions included clothes, a few dishes, and the small Ford truck that I bought in MN right before we moved to Michigan. Even though we didn't have much, I was determined to get my two older sons out of the conditions that were leading to an unthinkable outcome.

Locked Down
(Journal Entry)

January 13;
I've begun to write my story. I've begun to read a book. I play cards with other inmates, but I'm homesick. We called Mom-I tried to tell her how important it is for her to call Florida. (She now lives with my sister in Georgia) I don't think she knows what to do. I don't know what to do. Some of these people are nice, (in jail) some are scary, some are remorseful, and some are in another world. The guards are mean.

(The Story, 3)

The first thing I did after my brother's call was to get a steady job with benefits. Next, I proceeded to trade my truck for a used mini-van. Since the daring move I was preparing to make took time to prepare, I had months to think about how this family matter got so out of hand. Often times I hated myself for giving my Mother so much control over my kids' lives and mine. I also relived the pains and regrets that I felt when thinking of how me and the boys Father never really made it together. Oh, how his death pretty much meant that I was on my own trying to do something to get my kids back with me.

I was 18 when I had my first son. I was unmarried and basically homeless. My cousin let me stay with her, but I found out later, this would only be temporary. My Mother had long ago given up on her efforts to keep me under control, which meant that I had to leave the comforts of our family home. My arrogance and disobedient attitude finally burned that bridge right from under me. However, when Mom showed a caring attitude for my baby before he was even born, I was grateful, and I began to hope that we might learn to be decent toward each other. I really appreciated her help, as the baby's Father and me tried to see our way clear to be wed. In between our fights (which were very violent) and disagreements, I got pregnant again and I saw no way out but to abort. When it was over, I think we both felt so guilty that we felt that we had to get married.

Locked Down
(Journal Entry)

January 14;
I saw a squirrel-no a rabbit in the bushes across the street from the jail. It made me feel hopeful. I started working on a rap poem. (Just Another Case) Simply because I feel like I am being unjustly persecuted. I've had to readjust the way I take my pills because I am in constant pain. The concrete bed is getting to me now. I walk around the jail for exercise. I think I'm losing weight-that's good.

(The Story, 4)

After our wedding, which no one in my family attended, my Aunt gave us a small dinner at her apartment. Even though we were now married, we had no ideas on what to do next. We lived with his Mother for a short while and my Mother kept the baby most of the time. I was trying to work a minimum wage job, while my husband worked where he could and tried to pass the test to get his G.E.D. All though I was a high school graduate, I really had no direction and not enough training to hold a real job. In retrospect, I think me and my husband had a common problem of misdirected lives, which made us love each other in a strange sort of way. We met at the group home that focused on misguided kids and runaways. We tumbled through our lives together with an uncertain freedom that soon led us to another pregnancy when I was 20. He was 19 and determined as ever to get things in order by the time this baby was born. He appreciated my Mother's help, but he was growing tired of not having control of his family. In October, Jr. was born and we moved to a small efficiency apartment. Our fights and breakups were over, or so I thought.

About that time my parents moved to a small town in Florida and took my 2 year first born with them. I didn't feel bad about this because he stayed with them most of the time. When I look back to that time, I was living in a cautious attempt at a happiness we thought marriage life should have been. But my Husband couldn't a decent job and our frustrations served as the fuel that would always end in battle.

Just Another Case, (My Rap Poem)

THIS JUST ANOTHER CASE (WRONG FACE)

THIS JUST ANOTHER CASE (WRONG PLACE)

THIS JUST ANOTHER CASE (WRONG CHASE)

TELL ME!!WHERE IS MY REDEMPTION????

1...I'M LISTENING TO STORIES, SO MANY PAINS AND GLORIES

THE DRUGS, THE FIENDS, THE HIGH THE SCHEMES

THE LONGER THE NIGHTS, THE LOUDER THE SCREAMS

I'M FACING MY FEARS, I'M STOPPING MY TEARS

STILL, THERE'S HOPE IN MY SOUL

EVERYDAY I GROW OLD

NEVER LET GO OF THE PAST, HOPING IN JUSTICE TO FREE ME

AT LAST...NO PLACE FOR THE INNOCENT HERE

HERE THE INNOCENCE HOPE BECOMES THE CRIMINALS JEER

JEER CHEER ON TO THOSE WHO GET THEIR RELEASE

HOLDIN' ON TO THE HOPE, POSITIVE GOALS TO BE REACHED

AND THIS JUST ANOTHER CASE (WRONG PLACE)

JUST ANOTHER CASE (WRONG FACE)

JUST ANOTHER CASE (WRONG CHASE)

TELL ME!!!WHERE IS MY REDEMPTION????

2...MOVIN' ON WIT THE STORY, MORE FAME, NO MORE

GLORY

U SHACKLED AND CHAINED, ALL U GOT IS YO' NAME

SHOTGUN TO YO' BACK, JUST WAITIN' FOR U TO ACT

NEVER U MIND THE PANIC ATTACK, JUST STICK TO

THE FACT...GUILTY U BE, THAT'S ALL THAT THEY SEE

I DARE U TO TELL THEM THE TRUTH, THEY GONNA MAKE

A SAMPLE OF U

NOW THEY COCKIN' THEY GUN, NOW U WISH U COULD RUN

BUT THE FACT STILL REMAIN THAT U SHACKLED AND

CHAINED, SHACKLED AND CHAINED, SHACKLED AND

CHAINED...AND THIS JUST ANOTHER CASE (WRONG CHASE)

JUST ANOTHER CASE (WRONG FACE)

JUST ANOTHER CASE (WRONG PLACE)

3...AFTER SO MANY DAYS, AND IT'S FINALLY OVER

MADE IT OUT OF THE MAZE WITHOUT THE FOUR LEAF

CLOVER...

WASN'T IT LUCK THAT LOCKED ME AWAY NOTHIN' I DID

TELL ME SOMEBODY, WHERE WAS MY LUCK (I guess)
I GUESS IT RAN AND HID

Locked Down
(Journal Entry)

January 15;
The snow is melting, but the kids are still out of school. I'm glad. Denise won't have to drive my van. I don't like anyone to drive it. My cousin says that I'm too mean to my kids and I need to trust people-I don't trust anything-but God. Trust is what got me into this situation now-But Jah is my rescuer.

(The Story, 5)

Yes our violence toward each other increased in its intensity and in the severity produced broken bones. Our breakups became the only way we could find relief. Pretty soon, my second son was with my Parents at only a few months old. Time went by, and our children only lived with us between break-ups. Soon my Mother began to insist on the boys staying in Florida while we fought it out in Georgia. I started to agree with her. I wanted my babies to have a stable home, especially since I felt more and more unstable.

Finally, after a verbal confrontation between my Mom and my Husband that almost erupted in a brawl that my Aunt and cousin had to break up, my marriage was over. My kids went with their grandparents while I sunk into an area of self pity that even I didn't know awaited me.

Days passed and I struggled with my apathetic attitude. I questioned my willingness to let my kids go. I question my own sanity. With a tooth knocked from my beautiful smile, a broken bone in my face that Doctors elected to leave like it was. I wondered why our fierce relationship didn't end until he and my Mom almost came to blows.

Time kept moving and I felt like I was in a fog that wouldn't allow me to be or take optimistic steps to prepare for my responsibility of raising my boys as a single mother is supposed to. My brother Cedric helped me to get in an income based 2bedroom apartment and the fog started to lift. But my Mom played a counter move. She had adoption papers. Said she had to adopt my children so my Father's health insurance to cover their health. Another reminder of how much of a failure I was. I starred at the pictures she sent to show me what a stable and fun time the boys were having. Months went by and finally I resolved that this was best, and that the decision basically rested on my shoulders. My Mother and I seemed to get along now. I went to see my boys and sent money as often as I could. The 8-hour bus ride from Atlanta gave me time to reflect on the many emotions that were in constant conflict within my being. I felt guilty for what it meant for them to be away, and I felt relief too with no real responsibilities. The sky was the limit for me. I could work 2 jobs or 3 if I wanted. I started taking college courses at the local junior college, and I spent more time with my Grandma, who always encouraged me to do my best.

My freedom didn't last long, however. My brother, with whom I cherished a close relationship with, landed on my doorstep. He was somewhat of a drifter, in and out of jail and our lives, which made me glad to see him, and eager to move him in with me.

Later, I was saddened to find that not only did my brother have the aids virus, but also a fearless crack habit that showed me to a new level of what street life really meant. This was still early in the aids and crack epidemic that would soon shake our naïve world. My attention became fixed on keeping my beloved brother healthy and drug free. This was an uphill battle because he just didn't care and I didn't fully comprehend this fact until it was too late.

I still went to college and worked, but instead of concentrating on getting my life in order for my boys, I focused on the effects of the crack outbreak in my neighborhood. Looking back is almost as painful as the reality that enveloped me during those few heart-wrenching years.

After my Parents took my kids and my Husband and me called it quits for good, my life became to me, a moving picture. I felt like an outsider looking in on someone else's life. I came to a conclusion about myself at that time. All I had done since I was on my own was try new survival tactics that always depended on other people to be involved to support my plans. I held onto this man, not because I genuinely loved him, but simply to make the most of his resources for his own survival. No matter how meager his income was, I leaned on him to take care of us and be what he knew nothing about, and had no clue of where to start to learn to be what was natural, and true.

I still remember staring at the television when my Mom called to tell me that she had finalized the adoption papers. Now all I had to do was to sign the forthcoming papers and the sons I bore under the weight of my own sin would become my brothers. She promised that this was best for medical reasons and that she wouldn't deny my kids the right to know me. She just needed something to show the doctors. When she further suggested changing my baby boy's name, I didn't even flinch.

Locked Down
(Journal Entry)

January 16;
I am so angry with Denise. She does not seem to understand my predicament. Maybe she is glad that I have to suffer because I am always so arrogant. Maybe she thinks I deserve it. Maybe I do. Maybe now I will rely on God more and stop being so self-righteous. These dikes

make me want to love myself as I was created. My roommate is funny. She has an Uncle named Tadpole-her boyfriend is named Wiggy (ha-ha)

Locked Down
(Journal Entry)

January 17;
Nobody understands what it is like to be locked up.

Being locked up means no choices, no freedom, only humanity at the bare minimum. I spoke to all my boys' –earlier I cried when I thought of what Sunday means in my house. My babies are my life-they make me faithful to my God-Jah is my refuge.

(The Story, 7)

The entire area where we lived had quickly become, like many other low-income areas, festering places for crack addicts. I began to feel obligated to try and at least help my brother and the kids abandoned by their crack addicted Mothers. I became a listening ear for crazed women fighting an ever-controlling substance. I had nightmares about the kids I saw outside until the late hours in the night, wondering where their Mothers were. The stories about mothers selling their babies for a hit still makes me sad, especially when I realize that those children were perhaps the same age as my kids. My life was becoming a non-stop crusade. A hope that whatever I did would change someone's life for the better became my only objective.

My college life soon became my escape. My brother got closer to death and his drug use, which he said he needed to forget his pain. It was fast becoming too much for me to handle. I felt helpless and thus turned to my Parents to talk to him and make him want to fight to live. By the time we told them what was going on, it was too late and all they could do was take him to Florida where he would spend his final days in an anguishing and prolonged death. Aids claimed him as the disease seized the world in the 80's.

93

This tragedy proved to end my residency in my neighborhood also. I spent my last days there trying to do something worthwhile to speak out against the crack epidemic in my city. I worked with other organizations to have a parade for the kids who were profoundly affected by the drugs that isolated their Mothers and other relatives away from them. These kids were, for the most part, hardly ever considered in the war on drugs. I gathered as many as I could, and we made a banner, and proudly awaited our day to express the pain inflicted on us by the people we loved. We were bonded by the fact that we had to watch our dear loved ones literally self-destruct right before us. The pain was real, and the kids, (mostly boys) seemed to appreciate the union that we developed along the way.

Locked Down
(Journal Entry)

January 18;
Today my cousin is angry because the Power of Attorney I signed is not valid because it is not notarized. Then she says that I am argumentative and aggressive with my kids and Denise. But she adds that Denise is not being reliable. I am angry because nobody can help me-not even me. I keep praying that God will help me. Humans are dust...Got my Bible finally.

(The Story, 8)

Ironically, and sadly on the very day of the big parade, my brother passed away in my Mother's arms. The news of it tore at my soul. The guilt I felt because, once again, I had failed. I couldn't help him, and after the parade, I knew that these kids would go back to the same depressing place. I would be in Florida and unable to help them. My sadness rode with me and my brother's twin to say our last goodbye to possibly the best friend I ever had.

I later returned to Atlanta, only to find out that my 1st husband, (My kids natural Father) had died while I was gone. Aids was his enemy also. Missing the funeral made me feel even worse.

After all the grief had settled in, I drifted away from college, not to return, as sadness became my constant companion.

When I met my soon to be second husband, the African Prince, I began to hope in perhaps forming a new family. I figured that if I were to marry again, Mom and I could negotiate the kids living with us at least during the summer. After all, almost seven years had passed, and the boys were in school, and were quite accustomed to their life with their Grandparents.

Once again, though, I found myself seeking out new survival tactics that relied on someone else, and their resources. I not once believed that I was capable or even worthy of raising my boys by myself. It's not that I didn't have faith in my new Husband's ability to help me make a happy home. I just think that I really didn't give myself the opportunity to be what I really was; a single Mom.

When I found myself pregnant with my 3rd child, I was happy, but cautious. My Husband was still in college and constantly having to defend himself to me and our friends about his motives for marrying me. At the time, many people were getting married for immigration purposes only. Some of my friends told me that my African Prince had the perfect scheme because he had actually convinced me that he loved me. When he told me to abort our child, I was hurt deeply, but determined not to abort another child. The guilt would just to be too much. I remember telling my boys of the happy news of their new baby sibling. My youngest at the time cried, and reminded me that I had said that he would always be my baby. That's when I realized that my boys loved me for sure, and that they needed me as much as I needed them.

Locked Down
(Journal Entry)

January 19;
I started my countdown today. The jail here can only hold me for five working days. The MLK holiday stretched my wait for Florida to come and get me to about seven or eight days. Now I only have five more days to go. My roommate got out today, so I'm alone for now. I like that-my privacy is okay, although I kind of miss her. My cousin brought my two middle boys to visit. I was glad to see them, but now I'm really homesick. The glass between us makes me sad. I never thought my kids would see me like this-a common criminal is how I feel. Denise is really disrespecting my home. I thought she was my friend. This is why I don't trust people...

(The Story, 9)

In 1989, my African, born across the waters, was born. When I was alone with my new baby, I promised him and God that I would never be without him. I begged for help from the Almighty to teach me not to give up on being the best that I could be for this beautiful brown baby that I nursed with tears in my eyes.

The first few months of his life, his Father was still away finishing up his college career, so I had time to daydream and plan for the day when all my boys would be together with me and their new Daddy. The two oldest did appear to like him after all, and they were fascinated by his accent. This made me happy. When my parents came to visit, as they often did in the summer, the boys enjoyed their little brother, and tried to learn all of his African names.

Time went by slowly, and my anxious attitude reflected my dismay at the arrangements that existed before I even met my Husband. I loaded him down with my disappointment that things hadn't changed yet. He tried to understand, but his cultural upbringing would not bend to accept why my Mom and I had entered into such a precarious relationship.

Other people that I confided in concerning the situation told me that I was so willing to give my kids up simply because I had been given up as a baby. I strongly objected this notion, but in the back of my mind, I really was not sure. Meanwhile, I felt trapped by the fact of my own submission. I felt angry at my Mother for not letting my kids come and at least spend the summers with us. After awhile, I folded under the concept that they were legally her children now, and there was nothing that I could do about it. I had laid my bed, so to speak, and forced to lie in it.

Locked Down
(Journal Entry)

January 20;
This morning as I was dozing-the call came for me to be transported to Florida. Now, as I sit in my own clothes again, I wait. I wish I could just put on my coat and walk out of this place, but I just sit here reading and smelling my sweater. The smell of my laundry detergent is refreshing. It's now 8pm-been waiting since 9am. I wish they could come on.

(The Story, 10)

After my 3rd son was born, time seemed to fly. Before I knew it, it was 1992 and my Father was close to his final days on earth. We rushed to Florida to see him once more, and I embraced the fact that I was able to look at him and see him as well as I could see myself. My heart wept, as I understood from the love that I floated in deep in his dying eyes that everything must and will change. With my sister on one side of the bed, and me on the other, I rested my hand on his head. I received hidden treasures of this man that didn't father me from his sinewy anatomy, but rather from his unseen makeup. His essence, his wins and losses, his best and worse. I was sorry that my kids would not know their Father as I had known this man who gave me his name before I knew anything of the import of the issue. My consolation came from knowing that the boys benefited from growing up around my Dad and had received some of his wisdom and maturity from a lifetime of wear and wind.

I approached Mom again with the notion of allowing the boys to spend the summer with us. The answer was an emphatic NO! After our conversation, I felt bad for even asking her this during such a sad time. My Husband and I prepared to relocate to MN, and I left my home state unsure of when I would see my kids again.

(The Story, 11)

In Minnesota, I made plans and more plans for the day that all the kids would be together. The stress that resulted from my seemingly unrealistic hopes put a strong wedge between my husband and me. I expected him and his new corporate job to be a remedy of sorts. I spoke to lawyers, and counselors, all of which begged off when it came to such touchy family matters. Finally, depressed, and full of misplaced anger, my life was filled with uneventful days and shouting matches with my man at night. I don't think all our problems were the results of my Mother's situation, and me, but I do feel that it didn't help either. Sometimes average everyday worries for any married couple were exaggerated and made into something that neither one of us could recognize. The only place and time that we could find peace was when we were apart. Of course I would always beg for another try, ever determined to be content with what I had, always waking up with that empty feeling of the two that I did not know.

I often found myself staring at my birth certificate and wondering if my natural mother ever got that empty feeling. I wondered if she just gave me up with out a second thought. The one lesson I learned from this whole ordeal is: Always find a way to appreciate what is given to you. My Mom showed this to me. I found myself bitter at her, but not so bitter that I didn't learn from her. It became very clear to me that as the years moved on; she was determined to teach me something that she felt I needed from the beginning. Something I needed to undo the hurt and pain I felt toward my natural Mother. This woman, the only Mom that I knew, who had been adopted herself, and grew up in a time when such things weren't explored or talked about. She was old enough to be my grandmother when she adopted me, yet she still forced herself to take on more when her time for rest and relaxation was definitely in order. This Creole, this wife to my Father for almost fifty years, this dear woman, whom I still remember could do karate moves on me in her early sixties, spoke to me. She spoke to me, not with her mouth, but with her heart. She told me that even though she was not able to have children, she loved them, needed them, appreciated them, embraced them, and she knew that I would be the same say...once I found myself...my true self.

Well this wasn't the going to happen soon enough for me. I wanted an end to this ordeal, and I wanted it now!

Baby number 4 made me happy without a doubt. I named this one, and the struggle involved in his birth made me ever more aware of the love that existed between humans and their grand creator. I faced my fears, accepted myself, and walked away from my marriage, and my inner confusions, all together. The fact of triumph, the reality of truth, and the power of self-love and a true appreciation of life replaced the noise that clouded my way.

Upon arriving in Ohio, I felt fresh and finally, in the place where my Father's brother had lived and raised his family, I found the start of tranquility that I so desperately needed. Not like in Minnesota, where I was left with an emotional vacuum from never arriving to a passion that would never truly be mine. Ohio feels like an old shoe, comfortable yet reviving. My relatives still live in the same homes they lived in when I was but a youth, awkward and full of potential.

When my brother called with the report of what was going on in Florida, I can't say that I was completely surprised. As he made his report I let my mind go back to the last time Mama's horns and mind locked. We began the internal struggle of will. Where she left off, I was to pick up. First though, I had to trade my little Ford truck (Which I might add had been more that faithful during my journey from MN to OH) for a new pony. The "Transport" to be exact, would be my partner in the crime that would ultimately earn me a twenty-six (plus) day stay in jail. Not to forget my sincere accomplices and secret confidants who availed themselves to me, without judgment or questions.

I let my Mother know what I had done when I was far enough away that she could no nothing about it. I even let her know where I was and why I took the boys. It was left up to her as to what to do next. The younger of the two brothers cried immensely at the thought of his Nee-Nee being without him. His tears made me realize that no matter how much opposition I received from the family, I had taken the right step. I cried too, on the inside. I cried and worried because I had no idea of the consequences of my bold actions. All I could do was hope that the right thing, done in the wrong way would somehow find a balance. I felt strong, yet I bore the burden that was I had done was hurt my Mom, whom I love dearly, to the core. The only thing that made me feel okay was the flow of pure love that penetrated my senses with all my kids together. Each one exhibited a part of me, and each one loved me for their own special reasons. For the first time in my life, I saw myself; I mean I actually saw myself. Whatever days I've spent in jail and whatever is to come from now on cannot compare to the truth in what the gift of life really means.

Locked Down
(Supplemental Journal...Revisited)

January 21, 1999
It was well after midnight when the officers arrived. Equipped with shackles and leg chains, the female officer spoke as though we knew each other. With regrets I surrendered my shoelaces, my Bible, and everything else except the clothes on my back. I watched and choked back tears as my belongings were put into a plastic bag with my name misspelled on it. As I was being photographed, I wondered how I would express this experience on paper after it was over, whenever that would be. I was told not to ask how long the trip would be because I would not be told. This trip affected me in such a way that I will not soon forget. I tried to comfort myself by thinking and hoping that what I had done was right, and right always wins...right? I thought about conversations with my family over the preceding days. Part of the family felt that I had done the right thing in taking the boys, and the other part of the family felt that there were other ways to settle this matter. Either way, I was

the one stuck on a van going somewhere that I didn't know, for a seven day ride with no contact with my family for at least four of those days.

I think two days of picking up and dropping criminals went by before we stopped for an overnight rest. Some little jail in Indiana was where I was left alone in the drunken tank. I passed the time by reading the graffiti on the walls. I tried to imagine what sorts of people write so much about themselves in a place like that. Next, I tried to imagine just what my family was doing. Were they missing me? Were they worried? When would I return? These thoughts made me cry, and all I could do was try to sleep, and hope that my dreams would bring some solace to my troubled mind.

Waking up in a drunken tank, in a town unknown was unreal to me. I woke up thinking that I was at home in my own bed, wondering why my bed was so hard. I stared at the metal bed, with only my winter coat for a mattress for a moment. When I did realize where I was, I looked around to discover that someone had brought me a beautiful breakfast, all wrapped up in saran wrap. The toast, eggs, and bacon seemed to invite me to enjoy a few minutes of normalcy. I hesitated not to uncover the dish with an urgency that resembled the starved child of my past. This was the first decent looking food I had seen since my arrest. While on the road, all we were given was fast food burgers and water, and the jail food in Ohio was only for substance, not for taste. This breakfast would make up for all of that I thought while I tore off the wrapping. All of the thoughts in my brain halted when I was horrified to discover in this wonderful dish, a strand after strand of someone's hair carefully placed throughout the entire meal. I told myself that this was what I should expect from then on, and to expect otherwise would mean that I was disillusioning myself with hopes of decency that would not exist on this journey. From then on I would carefully inspect all food that was to pass through me on this venture.

The rest of the shackle and chain ride was much like being in a nightmare that was determined to finish before I woke up. Riding all day, with the guards and their shotgun as my guide, picking up and dropping off people all over the place, and never knowing where I was, began to make me feel kidnapped. I made a mental note of the attitudes of some of the criminals that were passengers. They seemed to look forward to going back to prison. It was almost as if they were going to be re-united with their families and friends. Some even bragged of their lives on the run, and how by some sudden turn, they were re-captured.

I wasn't sure of how much time passed when we held up for an overnight stay in a small jail somewhere in Kentucky. This time there were two other females in the small drunken tank with me. We had mats on the concrete floor, and one of the girls would flash the guards to get cigarettes and soda pop. After a while, the smoke and haze began to make me cough. I have long quit the habit due to the irritation of my bronchial system, after years of being addicted to nicotine. The other female, whose journey would take her to Texas eventually, was full of holes from body piercing. The three of us played cards and related our stories far into the morning. Before the guards brought our middle of the night breakfast, (4 or 5 am) the woman who was to join me on her way to another part of Florida, proceeded to stuff her tobacco possessions into her private parts. I promised, through gritted teeth to keep her secret, as she reasoned that she didn't know when she would get more for her addiction, and she had to do what she had to do.

Finally, our journey resumed, and I said farewell to the pierced up young lady. By the time we set out, it was about noon and I was beginning to feel hunger pains along with anxiousness to be where I needed to be to clear up this mess. I also worried for my family, whom I hadn't been allowed to speak to in at least three days. The guards too, seemed overly agitated. One constantly cursed a toothache, and the other spoke of dreams that warned her of inmates and their deception. She for this reason alone, doubled her probe of my person, and tightened my shackles extra tight. I felt even more apprehensive as the twelfth hour passed, and no stops were made to feed us, and I wasn't able to take much needed medication. Soon, my head was pounding, as the smoke filled the enclosed vehicle that seemed to race onward. The male passengers chained up in the back found unending ways to describe the filth and atrocities that awaited them. My ears felt like they were bleeding from the disgusting details that penetrated my thoughts. I drifted toward a slow, quiet panic, which took over my senses. When we did stop, it wasn't because I was pleading for food and medication, but to give relief to the other woman prisoner whose bladder was about to burst (I wonder why). When I was forced off the vehicle, being pulled by the chains that ruled me, I fell to the ground, unable to feel my own strength. I felt cold, yet I could feel sweat pouring from my brow. In the second it took for me to fall to the earth's freedom, the next second the air was filled with the sound of a shotgun being cocked by the male guard. I knew he was standing over me, with his gun positioned to damage me. Water burned in my eyes, and I was forced to breathe tears and anguish like never before. The steel part of me ran to an unknown corner and hid. No longer was I the bold person who had planned and carried out a kidnapping that I knew would bring pain and peace to my family, and to me. I shriveled up into a box of sheer mental panic and collapsed.

When I did come to my senses, we were going through my home state. I no longer felt the chains and shackles that held me, but more like a tour guide is what I had become. I explained to all the many beauties of my home. I reached down in my vocabulary to bring to them the best of what a proper upbringing had given to me. Suddenly, the male guard, to whom I had shown little concern to, lashed out at me and let me know that I was nothing to anyone, and that whatever pain that I had gone through on this journey, I fully deserved. Not only me, but also everyone who had the pleasure of of making his acquaintance. At first I thought, "How dare he". But as he rambled on, I realized that the problem was not I. I prayed that I would not take his assault personally, and my fever cooled as I told him that I liked him and that I thought that he was nice guy, no matter how much he hated his job. He continued to curse at me, but his words became like a wind of lost air, like that of a full balloon, blown up and let go to watch it go without any direction. When he was done, I felt his pain, as well as his relief in getting his true frustrations out in the open. Now, maybe he could heal.

I closed my eyes for a moment, and we were somewhere in the middle of Florida, where the tobacco-stashing female and we were left to wait for further transport. One thing I did take notice of while being locked up is that whatever is naturally beautiful in the state of a person's incarceration, it is kept from them. For instance, in Florida, the beauty of the sun is an everyday fact for the masses, something we often take for granted. When locked up, however, there is no more than a glimpse of the sun allowed at any given time. I'm sure that this is one of the many purposes of incarceration, but to someone who is quite used to freedom, in all its form, it becomes an odd situation. I found myself totally embraced by the small slit of a window where the sun seemed to linger just for my sad predicament and me. And why not I asked. Wasn't it I who basked in its rays while cutting the grass on the riding mower on my parents' property? Oh, how I enjoyed that one hundred-degree plus heat. It was as if the sun power seemed to energize me. Was it not me who enjoyed its heat on my back and face when walking through the small town that my parents chose to live without fear of those who would yell racial slurs while passing by? These are the thoughts that were going through my mind the morning I woke up to find myself somewhere in the middle of Florida. A gigantic black woman yelled at me, and I came to my senses. She was asking if I wanted by black-eyed peas. With an almost knee jerk reaction, I grabbed my plate, I'm a fellow southern girl, and no way was she or anyone else going to my hoppin john (peas and rice) This jail was more cordial than all the rest, and I quickly adjusted. The girls taught me how to sneak and make phone calls, and how to avoid the crazy one who shot her boyfriend just because he told her to. I was glad to be near a phone, which I immediately used to call my cousin. She told me that all was well and everyone was worried about me. With a smile of relief, I told the helpful inmates the good news. They breathed a sigh of relief also, like they were a part of my family too. The crazy girl too, had kind words for me. I became glad that such people did exist. This happiness did not last though. Ms Smoky in the Crotch began demanding that the girls give her their commissaries for her disgusting stash. The girls decided to reveal her revolting secret. I really didn't care except that it meant what we two were confined to an isolated area that had no working phone. I was very upset. I felt like grabbing this woman by her hair and hurling her off into space. Instead, I closed myself off. I decided then to just wait quietly for my redemption, which I felt was getting closer by the hour. The last time I saw her was 2 days later at supper. I told her to stop using drugs and to stop stealing, both of which imprisoned more than any jail could. She apologized for her actions, and I couldn't help but see in her the good that her own Mother must have seen on the day of her birth. I found myself holding on to the hope that her positive goals would be reached, someday. I slept deeply that night, with an early morning call to go on to my final destination. The woman was gone too, perhaps hours before me. I travel this road alone, I thought. The early morning dew settled on the ocean like the air that I could see dancing in the headlights of the prison vehicle that swayed at times due to a drowsy driver. His shotgun moved along ever so slightly in its holder. I watched the road go by and wondered if this image would ever leave me.

Now my court date, my freedom was fast approaching as I arrived in the small town where I had done my deed. As soon as I arrived and settled in, I told of my journey to a group of hard core listeners. These women were tough. They couldn't wait to let me know all about their death dealing, rough living, and time giving, lucky to be alive stories. I was grateful that my crime was more of a paper error than a true felony. But then something happened. As the days dragged on, these women began to crack. The one whom I recognized and labeled "The Weeper" wept nonstop, I got used to that right away. But the rest were a complete surprise. These women, one by one, began to crack. After that, the crying and sob stories went on and on. I wept also, but my tears were silent and secret. The toughest to the weakest slowly broke down. The bars, the loud toilets, the crowded conditions, all had something to do with the mental breakdown. I felt sorry for these women whose lives were a reminder of me of how much I had to be thankful for. No matter what I had been through, I knew what was at the end of this journey. The 4 children that I had carried inside me for the first months after their conception were happy in my daydreams, even though all of them earned punishments for their disobedience while I was away. After everything was over, I breathed the air like someone who had been locked away for years unjustly. I vowed not to take anyone for granted ever again. Sometimes when I'm angry about something that I can't control or is out of my hands, I glance up at the sky, seeing the moon or the clouds, and I smile a smile so deep that I know only me and God can feel.

On the way home on the bus that my extended family in Pensacola paid for, I hoped and prayed for all the people I met on my adventure. I hoped that these women, some who had never stopped in their lives to just...appreciate life, remain in my thoughts today. My record was cleaned up, as I was not convicted of any felony. The job that seemed so eager to have me labeled as a felon in order to relieve them from any further obligation to compensate me had to continue the payments and I went back to therapy.

My kids and I are still together, and now I am what I am, a single Mom. Thank you, God.

The Poet
I am the true poet, line by line

Verse is in me

Like grapes on a vine

Rhythm and rhyme as we do

Babble on

Words romance me like

A sweet, sweet song

Some may teach,

Or even amuse

Enlightening sometimes

And sometimes confuse

But words are a gift

How we use them is our

Choice

Hopefully to uplift

This is how we'll use

Our voice

So the next time you read a poem

Line by line

Think of the true poet

And how I thought of the rhyme

G.O.'97

I Was There

G.O.'1989

I was there

In the wee hours of the morning...

Watching the bodies sway

To music with empty lyrics

That somehow encouraged efforts of intoxicated minds

To have a good time

I was there

Listening to superficial conversations

As unreliable laughter filled the

Air...

Continuous attempts of relaxation in every mind

At hand

Led to the true essence of the meeting

I was there

Watching with pain, myself

Remembering with anguish, myself

Silently praying for another deliverance

I was there

Tell Me

Tell me, tell me, tell me
You love me, because I
Made you something
Something out of nothing

I'm biting my mails
Until they bleed
I'm biting my nails so
I can breath

I won't, I can't, I won't
Say that I love you
Even though we both know
That this love is true

Please step back and away
From my heart
I always do my best when
We're really far apart

Please, don't ask me
To come home I'll bring only heartaches
And lonely night alone

Tell me, tell me, tell me
Do you love me?
Someday, maybe, one day
But right now I'm free

G.1997

A Woman's Needs

I need a man...as gentle as a summer breeze

I need a man...one whose heart will never freeze

I need a man...to touch me like the morning dew

I need a man...who will help keep love new

I need a man...one who will never leave me alone

I need a man...one to make our house a home

I need a man...in my heart both day and night

I need a man...not Mr. Perfect, just Mr. Right

I need a man...who is not afraid of commitment

I need a man...he won't erase me like a misprint

I need a man...who can treat me like a queen

I need a man...he'll be the only man of my dreams

I need a man...do you fit? Are you the one?

I need a man...our happiness has only just begun

When I meet this man

He'll be my love, my life

My king

And

I will always need this man

And give him my all

My best, my everything

GO'98

Music, Sun, and Kids

I once saw a band of kids
    At play

As they enjoyed the rhythm of a beat
    Set before them

I couldn't help but to notice how
                Beautiful and happy

    The sun appeared
It danced with the melody explored

        Sure of themselves, they were not...
    That didn't matter though
            What was exceptional was

The music they played

        I felt invited to appreciate the talent

But the sun, it was something special that Day
        I just kept imagining that
The clouds wanted to play
        And the sun, it wanted to listen
To this band of children...

      Suddenly, when they rose to leave
            Their gig complete

I raised my Aunt's camera
And took a picture

Music, Sun, and Kids

My Tribute

TO ALL THE FOLKS WE'RE THINKING OF...

IN NURSING HOMES, HOME HEALTH WE LOVE

WE'RE GLAD YOU CAME ALONG...

YOUR STRUGGLES MAKE US STRONG

TO ALL THE FOLKS WE'RE THINKING OF...

TO ALL THE ONES WE TAKE CARE OF...

THROUGH ALL YOUR PAIN, STILL SHOW US LOVE

NO MATTER WHERE YOU'RE FROM

WE DEDICATE THIS SONG

TO ALL THE ONES WE TAKE CARE OF...

TO ALL THE PARENTS GREAT AND GRAND...
YOUR LIFE A STORY IN DEMAND

TRUE LESSONS THAT WERE LEARNED

AND NOW IT IS OUR TURN

TO ALL YOU PARENTS, TAKE YOUR STAND

TO ALL THE ONES WHO GAVE US JOBS...

FOR ALL THE KITCHEN FLOORS WE'VE MOPPED

ALL THE STORIES WE'VE EXCHANGED

SO MANY LIVES WITHIN THE FRAME

THANKS TO YOU WHO GAVE US JOBS...

AND NOW AS EYES MAY GROW SO DIM...
SWEET MEMORIES, REMEMBER WHEN
THE TIMES WE WON'T FORGET
THE FRIENDS YOU'RE GLAD YOU MET
THE LOVE YOU SHARED WILL NEVER DIM...

TO ALL THE ONES WE'RE THINKING OF...
IN NURSING HOMES, HOME HEALTH WE LOVE
NO MATTER WHERE YOU'RE FROM
WE DEDICATE THIS SONG,
TO ALL THE ONES WE'RE THINKING OF...

FROM; GENEVA OLOWOESHIN
C.N.A./H.H.A
SAINT PAUL, MN/DAYTON, OH

MY TRIBUTE

Tell Me (Remix)

Tell me, tell me, tell me you luv me

'cause you made me think I was somethin'

when I thought I was nothing

You thinkin', I'm thinkin', we thinkin'

I should leave, contemplating all the

pain and the games I don't need

I can't, I won't, I can't, I won't

Say that it's true

Even though you and me see

We know that I luv you

oooooh baby get back and step away

From my hart

But it's you that I miss whenever

We be apart

All you gotta do is just call

And I'm home

I'll be the cure for your heartache

No more lonely nights alone

When the time is right, I'll be the

One you need

We can dim the lights, I'm gonna set you free   GO'97

Reflections

Why God, why, do my offspring irate me with
Every breath they take
Why God, why, does a blue sky, and a cool breeze
Bring me to a calm state

Where oh God, where, are you when people are
Annoyed, with my silly and carefree
Demeanor
Where God, oh where, are you
Birds sing sweet melodies
Soprano and Tenor

When, oh God when, did my life seem to
Me not to matter, emotions suppressed
To avoid a panic
When, oh God when, did you see my value
In the womb of someone who's
DNA was probably manic

How oh God, how, do I keep living in a
World afraid, and mad
And those I thought would love me
Seem to have turned their back

How oh God, how, can you keep loving
Me, when I can't see truth in
Front of my face. Selfishly ripping a
Family apart to make my problems erase.

Who oh God, who am I to question your ways
When to me you've done no harm
And let me see many days,

Why I have survived, built to last.
What I have seen in this one day
Along with generations past
What I've seen and always is
That beauty, wisdom, and life
Overcomes pains and fears
While gentle breezes, and reflective moments
Fills our memories ears
G.O./...2010

Mama Went to Sleep

My Mother went to sleep in my arms, and still today I cry
Because she yet had something to teach me
Something to tell me why

She loved me so much, and I gave her my first born
For she herself was barren, so for every baby, she warmed

Who knew she'd live so long, after my Father's death
How she wept for him, many times, at the grave where he slept

But she pushed on, thanking the Good Lord
With every word she would say

And when the lights went dim,
We said goodnight
And beside my Father
She will faithfully stay

This Friendship

You say JUMP

          And I spring into action

      Hoping to gain your approval

Satisfaction

            I write words that I

Cannot, will not say

         So afraid to make your

      Smiles go away

I enjoy this friendship, it's like a chore,

It's hard to unlearn what was taught before

      But I see the outcome

            And I strive to be

The friend that I really am suppose to be

                                GKO2010

Sunrise

Beyond the columns and the trees

Closer to the oceans' breeze

The sun rises, and greets us,

In a most melodious way

It slowly and surely makes

For a new day

Whether to smiles, or to tears,

Motor engines sound

Our ears.

Whether slumber starts, or ends

A new day begins

Beyond the columns, and the trees,

Somewhere beyond the

Oceans' breeze

Sunrise

Genevakate 1998

This Morning

I awoke this morning with thoughts

Floating through

My head

Of how life

Is a

Journey of sorts

Times that make you and break you

Into many, many, pieces

We spend much time on this

Journey

Shaping and reshaping

These pieces and

Putting them back together

Only better and

Tighter and lighter

So as to continue on

Life's journey

Geneva2010

The Finalist

I've won, I've won!!!!!!

I think I won the competition!!!

But now as I wait for the final decision

I wonder,

I wonder deep down

Do I really deserve this crown?

Should I seek this special attention?

Or just settle for honorable mention

Will I be the one to get this prize?

Even though so many others tried

I've won, I've won!!!!

What a heavy load to bear

I've won, I've won!!!!

Thanks to all who give a care.

G.O.'97

Vision

It is in my vision that speaks to you

Yet my vision makes no sound
Above the hills it sweeps through you

To the homeless and to the

Homeward bound

It is my vision that cries to you

A simple plea that burns your ears

And chariots of Lexus and

Infinity

I yearn to ease my fears

It is my vision that makes me build

Unbreakable walls that grope

And capture the menacing purse of robbers

To destroy the deeds they hope

IIt is my vision that lifts me up

And speaks to you in kind

IIt is my vision that ever hopes

That the end of it we'll find

And together one day we'll smile

And remember the pain endured

It is my vision, the same as yours

Of a life peace has secured

Geneva K. Olowoeshin
2000

Love and Life...Life and Love

No matter how far and wide we travel

    Life move on and sometimes unravels

And sometimes stay put together

    In love and sweet divine

And sometimes we miss what we started

    But it's too late when love has parted

The waves of 2 oceans

    And love is sweet (contrite) and afraid

Of emotions (full of emotions)

    And love is something we want to hold

But oh how it hurts when it goes from hot to cold

    Yes love is as lovely as a bed of roses

That represents the best in life

    And in death is a door that closes

And love is a song with lyrics that plays on and on

And right or wrong love and life go hand in hand

    And without either of the 2 who could stand

And who would reprogram the reproductive

Process and who would hold our hand as we

Reached toward success

    And love can soothe the pain in the stories

That we tell and love will speak for us when our

Voices fail and love is what we most desperately need

    And need for always and forever like the air that we breathe

Yes love moves with the same rhythm as life and

We follow the streams of life and love together no

    Matter the details of how and however

No love is not our personnel to rearrange the

    Décor and the interior places and spaces

Of our world 'cause what matters to us most

Will sneak away from us like the unforgiving

Host

And we are never quite satisfied with best

    And yet our best can in fact be worst

But none of that flashes forth when we

      Finish first, in love and life

Cause love of life is still king...

Geneva K. Olowoeshin 2001   Get?It Productions

Get? It

I've been reading and writing
Since I was a child
Nappy afro,
Running free running wild

I skipped through school
Like a cool, cool breeze
Like writing poems and more poems
Under tall oak trees

Words and reading
I never grow tired
Of being enlightened
And deeply inspired

Poor Man, he tries to
Shut me down
'Cause I have survived
My strength, not from man
Even I'm pleasantly
Surprised...

Mother always said I was
I was the smartest of all
Words, not numbers
Is my very special call

So use the words that
Flow through this abandoned
Vessel...it's rich with truth
And blessed with treasure

If you are afraid of failing
If you let me in
I'll break down your fear
I'll patiently help us win

Prizes and Accolades
We don't need
To tell us we're gifted
Yet not the supreme

So I say to you once
And once more again
What's a poetry corner?
When the whole world's a fan.

had just approved federal $
the all-white Techwoc
project.
  Clara Lee Gibson, 70, $
been living in the housin$

A short summation including 3 pictures

OTHER SIDE OF PAGE INCLUDE ORIGINAL IMAGES OF OLD PROJECTS AND

GRANDMA KATE ON TOP UNDER HEADING "MY PEACH TREE IN THE PROJECTS"

Family Tree

With the help of Cousin Kate Boozer, we go back seven generations to her Grandfather and Grandmother Judson and Lucy Long (the Father of our Grandfather, Judson Long). Unto this Union 6 children were born. They are all deceased.

Uncle Mayor Long had fourteen children, two living.

Uncle Henry had nine children all deceased, grandchildren living.

Aunt Patsy Long Rutledge and fourteen children and one living, our Cousin Kate Boozer.

To most of us Grandfather Judson Long had ten children one daughter living, Aunt Patsy Harris.

Uncle Jim Long twelve children and two Daughters living, Vivion Sheroid and Ruby Smith.

Uncle Allen Long had four children and one living.

More than a hundred years ago Henrietta Brisco was married to Judson Long. From this married ten children were born (name in order of birth).

Wilber Long departed Oct.1930 he had seven children three living.

Jim Long depart April 1975 he all stepchildren.

Ada V. Long Ringer departed Jan. 1938 she had ten children, four living.

Anderson Long departed Dec. 1918 in the army no children.

Norman R. Long departed Nov. 1979 he had seven children and five living.

Robert Long departed Dec. 1975 he had six children and four living.

Ida B. Long Black departed Oct. 1979 she had seven children and six living.

Parrie Lee Long Jones departed Aug. 1976 she had only one son.

Patsy Long Harris is the only living relative from this immediate family, she has two children.

Nina Long (the baby) departed at a very young age Dec. 1931.

We are the fruit of the above families. And our children brings on another generation.

****
PROGRAM COMMITTEE

Minnie Long Jewsome   Della Long Wood
Tollia Black Frazier   Henrietta Black Rhodes
            Barbara Moton

The Summation

I know that there are many people writing, and sweating and hoping that every word they think of will perhaps be a best seller. I learned along time ago that I would live with the title of author only in my book. I began with the eager thought that everyone would be lining up to read what I know to be great literature. My best, my passion, and deliberate tones are unforgettable. I don't care if nobody even looks at my work, or even acknowledges my ability to write some of the most heart inspiring and mind piercing work that my generation has ever seen. I know I am good, and I don't need anyone to validate this. I have gone through life creating debt without any intention of paying it because I have known that I am a prodigy, an oddity, an invention, and named for a convention. In a hundred years this won't even be remembered. My very existence is an anomaly. I don't care about credit or what people with good credit can buy. They spend more time trying to train high prices dogs to protect the stuff from thieves anyway. I like to write, and that's the only thing I think of when I am not giving praise to my Creator. I live with a contentious and unpredictable personality that gets me in trouble and sometimes I get irritated with the process. I think of my origin and wonder who in this crazy world could have made this wonderful mistake. I write about the love of man and men in my life, but I must admit it has not been the merry-go-round I wish for. I have been slapped, spit on, verbally abused, permanently scarred, scammed, raped, discriminated against, choked, kicked, booed, made fun of, secretly witnessed unmentionable acts by, and finally, irreconcilably walked away from men for years. And just when I feel like I've walked the last tightrope in this world of dysfunctional make oriented journey, I realize one important thing. I am not afraid. I am not afraid of men. They don't intimidate me, no matter how much they berate me. I teach my fruit from my belly, (all MALES) to get to know themselves first, get to love themselves first. And during this process, they discover something astonishing; Mama. And then I become afraid, not of man, but of the Creator of man. One differs in the outcome of this reasoning. The circle of life is in tact with its failures, and triumphs. The molesters are molested, the wrongs are corrected, the cheats are cheated, the feared are made to be afraid, and with each sunrise, we all hope to make it the next sunrise with our hands and hearts clean. I read, and quietly scoff at the publishing companies who won't look at a new authors' work, passing on something great. The irritable wait. Continues. Fragments float in their own space. While I am waiting for my thoughts to gear me toward the writing process, I like to read short biographies. I read one of high regard once, and it became abundantly clear to me that while this author grew up in humble and impoverished circumstances; he still felt hurled into a place in life where he had to write. He had to show people that the thought of beauty not existing in the abandoned places is wrong. But he, like so many others who feel the desperation to validate their talent to the world, developed a death dealing habit and lifestyle that robbed him of the longevity of life needed to teach promising writers behind him how not to overrate themselves. His life struggles seemed to extend beyond his talent. This is what I have warned myself about many times as my life's journey is to lead me to be an opened book so to speak. I have taken my time and time again to reflect on what, and how I will approach the eventual success that this venture and others Get?It Productions will lead to. That's why I like to think of all I do and ask others if they get it. Yesterday I didn't get it, today I may not get it, but tomorrow or maybe later in the future, I will get it. I will get the fact that this project will end. I pray for a finish to this writing as I wonder where it will end. I get that the ending may just be the beginning of a new story.

I am not a poet
At least
Not an original
One
The most beautiful
Words
I've seen are
In the
Proverbs
And
Psalms

Gkate2010

The Sum of something=something else...Get? It

136